Incisive   *Cities*

"Another   *a is."*

Robert D. Reed Publishers • San Francisco, CA

Robert D. Reed Publishers
750 La Playa, Suite 647
San Francisco, CA 94121
Phone: 650-994-6570 • Fax: -6579
E-mail: 4bobreed@msn.com
web site: www.rdrpublishers.com

Typesetter: **Barbara Kruger**
Cover Designer: **Julia Gaskill**

ISBN 1-931741-34-4

Library of Congress Control Number 2003092479

Manufactured, typeset and printed in the United States of America

Dedication

For Steve, my first traveling companion, and Monica, my last.

Contents

Alabama

Quips & Quirks

Birmingham

"Birmingham is, I believe, the most beautiful industrial city in America. The downtown is neat and modern, and the residential sections are superb. The only thing I don't like about Birmingham is that when you blow your nose in the morning you wonder if you haven't been out cleaning chimneys in your sleep." —journalist Ernie Pyle, March 3, 1938

Montgomery

Bus Boycott—On December 1, 1955, a tired maid named Rosa Parks refused to give up her seat in the front of a Montgomery bus. Local pastor Martin Luther King organized a successful bus boycott that marked the beginnings of the civil rights movement.

Alaska

Quips & Quirks

From the Internet: You Live in Alaska When…
You only have four spices: salt, pepper, ketchup and Tabasco.
Halloween costumes fit over parkas.
You have more than one recipe for moose.
Sexy lingerie is anything flannel with less than eight buttons.
The four seasons are: winter, still winter, almost winter, and construction.

Anchorage

"Please don't write another article about how 20-year-olds can come up here and make $50,000 a year fishing." —Chamber of Commerce receptionist to travel writer Jack Bettridge during his research for "The 10 Best Places To Live," July 1996 *Swing*

"People come here to get away from it all. It's like another country, where everyone happens to speak English." —Jed Miller, University of Alaska at Anchorage graduate student, quoted in "The 10 Best Places To Live," July 1996 *Swing*

"The odds are good, but the goods are odd. We're talking about a lot of mountain men." —Christine Williams, University of Alaska at Anchorage student, quoted in "The 10 Best Places To Live," July 1996 *Swing*

Attu

Nosy Neighbors—Russia's easternmost point is just 55 miles away from Attu, the westernmost Aleutian island, making it the closest noncontiguous country to the U.S. Briefly held by the Japanese, was also the site of only ground fighting of World War II to take place on American soil.

Barrow

Will Rogers' Final Destination—Will Rogers and Wiley Post took off from an Eskimo village bound for Point Barrow when the engine of their small plane conked out, sending the plane into a frozen riverbank and killing them both on August 16, 1935.

Fairbanks

"The legendary cold of Fairbanks cannot compare to the warmth of its people." —Golden Days legend "Miss Ricki" Chagnon

"The backyards are bigger than the largest park I've seen in New York." —mountain biker Rachel Kanz

"To live in Fairbanks, Alaska, and sculpt ice is the equivalent of a stone sculptor in Italy within sight of the marble quarries." —ice sculptor Steve Brice

Kodiak

"Kodiak may not be at the end of the world, but you can see it from there." —unknown

Nome

"We don't like rules. We don't like regulation. We don't like government intervention." —Laura Kosell, director of the local museum

"People call here and think we're the capital of the State just because they've heard of Nome more than Juneau." —Lois Wirtz, head of the Nome Convention and Visitors Bureau

Skagway

"That's the most unrealistic thing about *Northern Exposure*. This town would not tolerate an obnoxious little jerk like [Rob Morrow's character Dr. Joel Fleischman]." —Skagway resident Scott Logan, quoted in the September 28, 1992, *Atlanta Journal and Constitution*

Arizona

Quips & Quirks

"Arizona doesn't observe daylight saving time because there's no point in saving an hour of 112-degree daylight." —Thomas Kunkel in a profile of Fife Symington, April 1997 *George*

Four Corners—The only place in the U.S. where four states meet is the spot where Arizona, New Mexico, Utah, and Colorado come together.

Longer Than St. Augustine—The Hopi village of Oraibi is the oldest continuously inhabited town in the United States.

From the Internet: You Live in Arizona When...
- You think temperatures in the 90s means it's cooled off;
- You don't know why anyone would own an umbrella, raincoat, or overcoat;
- You've signed petitions to require drug testing and mental competency examinations for state legislators;
- You know the difference between a tamale and an enchilada, but not between a crepe and a quiche;
- The most ice you've seen in one place was a Margarita;
- You've killed for a shaded parking space.

From Tucson resident George Newman: It's So Hot In Arizona That...
- The birds use pot holders to pull worms out of the ground.
- Farmers feed their chickens crushed ice to keep them from laying hard-boiled eggs.
- The cows are giving evaporated milk.
- The trees are whistling for the dogs.
- A sad Arizonan once prayed, "I wish it would rain—not so much for me, cuz I've seen it, but for my 7-year-old."
- You no longer associate bridges (or rivers) with water.
- You eat hot chiles to cool your mouth off.
- You can make instant sun tea.
- You learn that a seat belt makes a pretty good branding iron.
- The temperature drops below 95, you feel a bit chilly.
- When the temperature drops to 102 in July, the weather forecaster talks about a cooling trend.
- You discover that in July, it takes only two fingers to drive your car.

- You discover that you can get a sunburn through your car window.
- You notice the best parking place is determined by shade instead of distance.
- Hot water now comes out of both taps.
- You actually burn your hand opening the car door.
- You realize that asphalt has a liquid state.

Grand Canyon

"Here, I find the same atmosphere as at Niagara Falls: the most ingenious efforts have been made to transform a natural marvel into a kind of amusement park." —philosopher Simone de Beauvoir, March 17, 1947

Phoenix

"In Egyptian mythology, the phoenix was a majestic bird that lived in the desert for half a millennium before consuming itself by fire and rising renewed from the ashes. Though by Egyptian standards, Arizona's Phoenix has 400 years left to smolder, newcomers desperate to acclimatize after an air-con arrival may well believe that their goose is cooked." —*www.lonelyplanet.com*

Tucson

"One of the glories of Tucson is its early morning light... People in Tucson come to appreciate the early of that early light, as wine drinkers appreciate a special bouquet." —author Larry McMurtry, *Roads: Driving America's Great Highways*

Arkansas

Quips & Quirks

"Arkansas drivers, of all drivers in America, are the least likely to yield the fast lane. They just won't let you by. This is not because they are macho, it's because they're indifferent to even such modest subtleties of the road. To Arkansas drivers, the lanes look the same and are treated the same." —author Larry McMurtry, *Roads: Driving America's Great Highways*

California

Quips & Quirks

"I cannot conceive of anything more ridiculous [than] that we are profiting by the acquisition of New Mexico and California. I hold that they are not worth a dollar." —Daniel Webster, speaking on the floor of the Senate in 1848; ten days after Mexico ceded California to the United States, gold was discovered at Sutter's Mill

"The name is almost as magical as New York. It's the land of streets paved with gold, of pioneers and cowboys. Through history and movies it's become a legendary country that, like all legends, belongs to my own past... It is the only state, I'm told—along with Texas, perhaps—that thinks of itself as California before feeling it's part of the U.S.A." —philosopher Simone de Beauvoir, February 25-26, 1947

"California is a place in which a boom mentality and a sense of Chekhovian loss meet in uneasy suspension; in which the mind is troubled by some buried but ineradicable suspicion that things had better work out here, because here, beneath that immense bleached sky, is where we run out of continent." —Joan Didion in "Notes from A Native Daughter," from *Slouching Toward Bethlehem*

"Everywhere they say, 'Go to California! California's the great pot o' gold at the end of the rainbow.' Well, now we're here in California, and there ain't no place else to go, and the only pot I seen's the kind they peddle at Sixtieth and Avalon." —a Watts rioter, 1965, quoted in Curt Gentry's *The Last Days of the Late, Great State of California* (still one of the most incisive books ever written about the state)

"[Northern California] as we all know, is the undisputed center of the universe and the only decent place left on the planet. (Civilization as we know it stops at Lee Vining to the east and Hearst Castle to the south. All else is vast wasteland full of shoe salesmen, movie stars and chicken farmers.)" —*San Jose Mercury-News* travel editor Zeke Wigglesworth, October 1996

"Everything worth photographing is in California." —photographer Edward Weston

"In full honesty, California does have everything. And we are sad at leaving because, in the way of all things, no man knows but that this backward glance over the shoulder may be his last glance forever." —journalist Ernie Pyle, November 17, 1939

"Religious belief here isn't lacking or even vague, it is creative and questing. It's also a reasonable alternative when materialistic satisfactions aren't available. A person who works hard every day and lives in a single room but is surrounded by a world of friendliness, beauty, sunshine, and sensual delight might well turn away from the institutionalized religion of success and conformity." —novelist Jane Smiley, "California is Worth It," June 16, 2002, *San Jose Mercury-News*

From the Internet: You Live In California When...
* You make over $250,000 and you still can't afford to buy a house.
* The high school quarterback calls a time-out to answer his cell phone.
* The fastest part of your commute is going down your driveway.
* You know how to eat an artichoke.
* You drive to your neighborhood block party.
* When someone asks you how far something is, you tell them how long it will take to get there rather than how many miles away it is.

Hold the Territory, Please—California is the only state to join the Union without ever having been a colony or a territory.

That's Mass Transit—The longest municipal rail transit system in the country once covered some 1,200 miles in southern California; it was torn up after World War II.

Bakersfield

Oil Field Scandal—The great scandal of the Harding Administration revolved around members of the Cabinet leasing oil to private companies that was supposed to be kept in reserve for the military. The oil in question was stored at Elk Hills, near Bakersfield, and at Teapot Dome in Wyoming, which gave the scandal its name.

Berkeley

"It is ultimately the people of Berkeley—those same irritating frowners and scolders, those very neurotic geniuses and rapt madwomen—whom make this place, who ring an endless series of variations on its great theme of personal and communal exploration, and who, above all, fight tooth and nail to hang on to what they love about it." —novelist and resident Michael Chabon

Carmel

"If Carmel's founders should return, they could not afford to live there, but it wouldn't go that far. They would be instantly picked up as suspicious characters and deported over the city line." —John Steinbeck, *Travels with Charley*

"Carmel, you know, is the West Coast art colony—the Greenwich Village of the Pacific, some have called it… The architecture is a pleasant hodgepodge. Private homes are New England farmhouses, and low English cottages, and beachy places, and jutting Pueblo Indian, and there's the Mexican theme, and even straight Hollywood Spanish. Nearly all are beautiful and livable-looking. I have seen only two or three mansions, and they were grotesque amid the soft quietness of the town. Their owners should be ashamed, but probably aren't." —journalist Ernie Pyle, November 16, 1936

Death Valley

"There is nothing consistent about the valley floor. I have driven the whole hundred-and-thirty miles, and there is hardly a five-mile stretch that is the same. Some places it is sand. Some places very gravelly, with good-sized rocks. Some places actually swampy. Some places hard and black, like old lava. Some places snow-white—salt beds, just as in Utah." —journalist Ernie Pyle, March 23, 1938

"No landscape ever seemed to me as overwhelming on screen as these plates of salty earth, cut by deep crevasses and stretching to infinity between walls of fire. I never even dared to dream of touching them, yet I am touching them, and in the startling truth of the setting, the drama itself becomes real: I believe in the agony of von Stroheim's heroes [in the film *Greed*]. The depth of this valley frightens me." —philosopher Simone de Beauvoir, March 10, 1947

Eureka

"I don't care how widely traveled you are, nobody has really seen all of America until he has driven through the redwood forests… You don't feel they're trees at all. You feel as if they're something half human and half ghost. Everybody I've ever talked to has had that queer feeling about driving through the redwoods. You wouldn't be surprised to see an immense, gnarled wooden hand reach out and snatch you away into nowhere." —journalist Ernie Pyle, October 10, 1939

Hollywood

"Hollywood is a town where everyone wishes everyone else will fail, and if you die in the process, that's even better." —producer Jeffrey Katzenberg

"They have great respect for the dead in Hollywood, but none for the living." —actor Errol Flynn

"It is the executive who decides to 'take' the meeting, plucking a screenwriter from a large pool of supplicants as Nero might have plucked an apricot or a plum from a basket of fruit. As India has its untouchables, so Hollywood has its untakables, human fruit so spoiled by failure or treachery that no executive is likely to accept it." —author Larry McMurtry, *Roads: Driving America's Great Highways*

"If God doesn't destroy Hollywood Boulevard, he owes Sodom and Gomorrah an apology." —comedian Jay Leno

"I hate Hollywood as a place just as I did before. It's overcrowded, vulgar, cheap, and sad in a hopeless sort of way. The people on the streets are all tense, eager and suspicious, and look unhappy—the has-beens and the would-bes." —author Ayn Rand, whose first job in America was working as a scenario writer for Cecil B. DeMille, after writing the screenplay for *The Fountainhead*

"Thirteen years ago, when he stayed here on his first trip to Hollywood, architecture had seemed to be an extension of the studio back-lot with private homes disguised as Norman castles or Oriental mosques, with gas stations built to resemble medieval towers, and movie houses that took the form of Egyptian temples or Chinese pagodas. In that lavish heyday of the parvenu, when everything was built to look like something it wasn't, a bungalow court with accommodations indistinguishable from a hundred other bungalow courts came to be known as the Garden of Allah." —from Budd Schulberg's *The Disenchanted,* a roman à clef of F. Scott Fitzgerald's last days in Hollywood

"There is in Hollywood, as in all cultures in which gambling is the central activity, a lowered sexual energy, an inability to devote more than token attention to the preoccupations of the society outside. The action is everything, more consuming than sex, more immediate than politics, more important always than the acquisition of money, which is never, for the gambler, the true point of the exercise." —Joan Didion in *The White Album*

"When you're from Hollywood, it's a world of fantasy. When you live in a world where illusion is more important than the truth, that affects your perception." —Harland Braun, one-time attorney for actor Robert Blake, attacking the prosecution witnesses' veracity

First Film—In 1913, Cecil B. DeMille wanted to shoot his first motion picture, a Western, in Flagstaff, Arizona, but he found it too mountainous. Looking for a better landscape, he headed west and ended up in a small agricultural town called Hollywood.

Huntington Beach
"Legend has it that Jan and Dean's '63 anthem [Surf City] was inspired by Huntington Beach. Think of '60s surf mania as a tactical nuclear strike aimed at buttoned-down Middle America, and Huntington Beach as ground zero." —Peter Fish, *Sunset Magazine*

Long Beach
Spruce Goose Loose—The only time Howard Hughes' flying boat, the 200-ton Spruce Goose, flew was for one mile across Long Beach harbor on November 2, 1947. The $7 million craft was warehoused after that flight because of government investigations into war contracts.

Los Angeles
"The real Los Angeles cannot be seen because it is to be fond only in such invisible qualities as newness, openness, freedom, variety, tolerance, and optimism, and of course the weather – which is visible only when it's bad." —*Los Angeles Times* columnist Jack Smith

"Where the freeways of Los Angeles are concerned, the wise man takes nothing for granted. It takes a while to land at LAX, debark, secure a rental car—twenty minutes at least. In that length of time a bobble or small accident almost anywhere in the system—on the 10, on the Harbor Freeway, on the 405 itself—can bring all traffic within ten miles to a sullen halt." —author Larry McMurtry, *Roads: Driving America's Great Highways*

"What I now hate are the great garages—these garages have replaced security guards as the main threat to the serene life of the screenwriter. In Century City particularly these garages are Dantesque, leading one inexorably down, level by level, into a hell of whiteness, in which all the parking spaces seem to be reserved, either for the legions of the handicapped or for the even more prolific legions of executives, somewhere in the tower above you, for whom a secure parking space is simply one of the perks of the job." —author Larry McMurtry, *Roads: Driving America's Great Highways*

"The capital of the Third World." —author David Rieff

"A former movie actor was running for governor again and supporting a former tap dancer who is defending his Senate seat against the son of an ex-heavyweight champion of the world. It was just an ordinary day in Los Angeles." —from Bill Moyers' 1971 book, *Listening to America,* commenting on Ronald Reagan supporting George Murphy in his race against Gene Tunney's son John

"Of course he's guilty. Please! They have the murder weapon, the motive, two witnesses, 900 pieces of evidence. But hey, this is L.A. You're going to need more than that to convince the jury." —comedian Jay Leno on actor Robert Blake's murder trial

"Just as northern California wants no part of Los Angeles, a good-sized chunk of Los Angeles now wants no part of Los Angeles either." —unidentified pundit on the San Fernando Valley secession movement

"All the neighborhoods we drive through are either disorganized outlying districts or huge developments where identical wooden houses multiply as far as the eye can see, each one surrounded by a little garden. The traffic is terrifying; the broad roadways are divided into six lanes, three in each direction, marked off by white lines, and you are allowed to pass to either the right or the left." —philosopher Simone de Beauvoir, February 25, 1947

"I don't want to live in a city where the only cultural advantage is that you can make a right turn on a red light." —Woody Allen as Alvy Singer in *Annie Hall*

"If I can convince Norman that Los Angeles is part of the United States, it shouldn't be a problem." —Katharine Hepburn as Ethel Thayer, responding to an invitation from daughter Chelsea in *On Golden Pond*

"As a kid in Los Angeles, I grew up in a film-industry community, and it didn't have that Holy Grail appeal that it has for some people. I was there and I was not impressed." —Robert Redford

"Fortunately, the freeways are moving. Unfortunately, the cars on them are not." —KNX DJ Jim Thornton during an aftershock of the January 1994 Northridge earthquake

"L.A. is always ignored. It accentuates the phlegmatic nature of the town, the disassociation of people from their community, the indifference or torpor of its elites," Joel Kotkin, author of *The New Geography: How the Digital Revolution Is Reshaping the American Landscape,* on how the major media being based on the east coast affects the city.

Marin County

"It's Marin County. We're all Buddhists up here." —film director George Lucas

"Driving Highway 101 in what you might call bummer-to-bummer traffic has taken the place of 'mellowing out.' Road rage is commonplace. If Marin had an official bird, it would be the raised third finger." —novelist Cyra McFadden, May 26, 2002

Mojave Desert

"The Mojave is a big desert and a frightening one. It's as though nature tested a mean for endurance and constancy to prove whether he was good enough to get to California." —John Steinbeck, *Travels with Charley*

Monterey

"It is a beautiful place, clean, well run, and progressive. The beaches are clean where once they festered with fish guts and flies. The canneries which once put up a sickening stench are gone, their places filled with restaurants, antique shops, and the like. They fish for tourists now, not pilchards, and that species they are not likely to wipe out." —John Steinbeck, *Travels with Charley*

"There are many picturesque spots, orange or apricot walls, arbors, and painted inns, but the effect is a little like part of a museum, and you still feel you're in the U.S.A." —philosopher Simone de Beauvoir, March 2, 1947

Oakland

"Only in Oakland would a man get a standing ovation for stealing something." —unknown San Francisco Bay Area DJ, commenting on the crowd's reaction after baseball player Rickey Henderson stole his 939th base, breaking Lou Brock's record.

"After the 1906 earthquake, tent cities sprang up in every park, and hot food stations were hammered together out of canvas and boards on street corners, ladling out bowls of Irish stew, bread and tea to the refugees. A sign over one station read: 'Eat, Drink and Be Merry, for Tomorrow we may have to go to Oakland.' Another person asked why San Francisco had been destroyed while Oakland was intact. 'There are some things even the earth won't swallow,' came the reply." —from David Siefkin's *The City At the End of the Rainbow: San Francisco and Its Grand Hotels*

"You can go anywhere out through the Golden Gate—to Australia, to Africa, to the seal islands, to the North Pole, to Cape Horn… Oakland's just a place to start from, I guess." —from Jack London's *The Valley of the Moon*

Earhart Departure—Amelia Earhart took off from **Oakland** on May 21, 1937, heading east on an historic round-the-world flight. In early July, just three stops (Howland Island, Honolulu, San Francisco) from completion, she and her navigator Fred Noonan disappeared.

Palm Springs

"This place is like the Gay '90s. Everyone here is either gay or in their 90s." —a local denizen, 1995

Palo Alto

"To attempt to establish a great university Aladdin-like out of nothing but money is as useless as would be the building of a great summer hotel in Central Africa, or an institution for the relief of destitute ship captains in the mountains of Switzerland." —1891 *New York Commercial-Advertiser* editorial pooh-poohing Leland Stanford's plans to establish a California university in honor of his late son

"If you've been to Ithaca, N.Y., you know that Palo Alto is no Ithaca. Nor is it Eugene, Princeton, or State College. It is definitely not Berkeley. Perhaps that's a plus. However, the comparisons to the hometowns of Cornell, University of Oregon, Princeton, Penn State and Cal make it clear

that Palo Alto comes up short in one significant way: it's no college town."
—Mark Simon in the April 2002 *Stanford*

Largest Football Stadium—With a capacity of 85,500, Stanford University's stadium is the largest at a private university in the U.S.

Sacramento

"In Sacramento, it is fiery summer always, and you can gather roses, and eat strawberries and ice cream, and wear white-linen clothes, and pant and perspire." —Mark Twain

"The capitol, a smaller version of the one in Washington, stands at the back of a park, amid lawns and trees. In modern cities, trees are confined to gardens, but her they invade the avenues, where the smell of plants and the silence are surprising; they form a thick vault above the central boulevard, which is lined with beautiful old wooden houses. I love their elaborate architecture—the gables, the porches, the verandahs. I love their dusty colors. One expects to see old gentlemen in silk hats and women in crinolines descending the steps." —philosopher Simone de Beauvoir, March 7, 1947

Beginnings—Natives of Sacramento include author Joan Didion and actors Timothy Busfield, Ray Collins, and Molly Ringwald.

San Diego

"If Los Angeles is the city most Easterners think of when they think California, San Diego is the city they dream of when they dream California." —Neil Morgan, *San Diego Union-Tribune* columnist

"San Diego's superb coastline, near-perfect climate and Mediterranean facade make it the quintessential Southern California beach city. Forget the pace and pollution of LA—if you want to wet your feet in the So-Cal beach scene, pull on your kneebangers and start styling with the boardheads or shopping for rugs and real estate in affluent, conservative, blessed-by-nature, merging-with-Mexico San Diego." —*www.lonelyplanet.com*

San Francisco

"Insanity, as might be expected, is fearfully prevalent in California. It grows directly out of the excited mental condition of our population, to which the common use of alcoholic drink is a powerful adjunct." —Dr. Henry Gibbons, speaking before the San Francisco County Medical Society, January 27, 1857

"It's the indescribable conglomeration of beauty and ugliness that makes San Francisco a poem without meter, a symphony without harmony, a painting without reason—a city without an equal." —from Herb Caen's October 22, 1940, *Chronicle* column

"San Francisco is Boston without the weather." —marketing consultant Noreen Theede

"In L.A. you're one of 10,000 screenwriters driving the same streets, meeting the same people, eating at the same restaurants…having the same experiences. I'm trying to write some dark stories. So San Francisco weather—the rain and the fog—is good. Good for the psyche. Mine, anyway." —screenwriter Ehren Kruger *(Arlington Road)*

"San Francisco was a revelation to me. I had thought every city west of Chicago was a Hackensack. San Francisco convinced me that I would have to revise my concept of Western metropolises. San Francisco looked to me like New York with a hill in the middle of it." —comedian Fred Allen, upon arriving in 1915 while on the vaudeville circuit, as noted in his autobiography *Much Ado About Me*

"San Francisco is a shockingly stubborn abstraction, a geometric delirium. The plan was traced on paper without the architect even glancing at the site. It's a checkerboard pattern of straight lines and right angles, just as in New York or Buffalo. The hills, those very material obstructions, are simply denied; the streets scale up them and hurry down without deviating from their original design." —philosopher Simone de Beauvoir, March 3, 1947

"Nobody trusts us. When the S.F. Actors Theater applied for the rights to do Clare Boothe Luce's play, *The Women,* at the Zephyr Theater on Van Ness, the contract arrived from N.Y. with a message from Mrs. Luce specifying that all 35 female roles MUST be played by females!" —from Herb Caen's June 16, 1986, column

"As a physical center of people, [the Haight-Ashbury] worked like a cyclone—tugging them in from all over, whirling them up in the air and scattering them in every direction." —author Charles Perry in the concluding chapters of *The Haight-Ashbury, A History*

"San Francisco could take it easy if it wanted to. It could just sit there on the apron of the continent and find contentment in its unfair share of splendor. But America's most hypersensitive city has never been happy without a cause to embrace passionately or, at the very least, something to be ticked off about." —columnist Steve Lopez in the August 11, 1997, *Time,* discussing the war between bicyclists and drivers

"I suppose there are cities more sophisticated, with a better climate, more cultural attractions and a more tolerant attitude toward life, but surely none can combine all those qualities the way San Francisco does." — syndicated columnist Donald Kaul

"Only in San Francisco would you find them making a movie where the male lead is named Mandy and the female lead is named Glenn." — unknown wag commenting on the 1985 production of *Maxie,* starring Glenn Close and Mandy Patinkin

"If, as they say, God spanked the town,
For being over-frisky,
Why did He burn His churches down,
And save Hotaling's whiskey?"

—written by Charles Field after his discovery of an undamaged liquor warehouse on Jackson Street after the 1906 earthquake

"We wandered around, carrying our bundles of rags in the narrow romantic streets. Everybody looked like a broken-down movie extra, a withered starlet; disenchanted stunt-men, midget auto-racers, poignant California characters with their end-of-the-continent sadness, handsome, decadent, Casanova-ish men, puffy-eyed motel blondes, hustlers, pimps, whores, masseurs, bellhops—a lemon lot, and how's a man going to make a living with a gang like that?" —from Jack Kerouac's *On The Road*

"The afternoon sun painted her white and gold—rising on her hills like a noble city in a happy dream. A city on hills has it over flat-land places. New York makes its own hills with craning buildings, but this gold and white acropolis rising wave on wave against the blue of the Pacific sky was a stunning thing, a painted thing like a picture of a medieval Italian city which can never have existed." —John Steinbeck, *Travels With Charley*

That was Fast—Yankee Joe DiMaggio married actress Marilyn Monroe at San Francisco City Hall on January 15, 1954, and filed for divorce there nine months later.

Clipper Service—Pan American Airways inaugurated its China Clipper seaplane service from Treasure Island in San Francisco Bay with a Sikorsky S-24 plane, known as a "flying boat," on April 16, 1935.

Harding's Last Gasp—Falling ill after eating tainted crab in Alaska, President Warren Harding died on August 2, 1923, in the presidential suite on the seventh floor of the Palace Hotel on Market Street. His western itinerary was to include a visit to Stanford University, but because of his death—which some thought was actually murder—he remains to this day the only Republican president never to visit that university.

It Didn't Really Happen—There is a plaque on the side of the building at the corner of Bush and Stockton Streets that notes, "On this site Brigid O'Shaughnessy killed Miles Archer." What the plaque doesn't say is that O'Shaughnessy and Archer are fictional characters in Dashiell Hammett's *The Maltese Falcon*.

San Jose

"People in Silicon Valley have what only a few places in America have, which is a myth to call their own. New York has one, Los Angeles has one, Texas does, and maybe Detroit and Chicago. The people in Silicon Valley believe they live where the future is being born." —Jamie Malanowski in the September 1997 *Time Digital*

Radio Started Here—The world's first radio station began broadcasting in San Jose at the corner of First and San Fernando Streets in January 1909. When licenses were first issued in 1921, owner Charles David Herrold took the call letters KQW. The station was purchased by the Columbia Broadcasting System in 1949 and moved to San Francisco, where it still broadcasts today as KCBS. (Many people believe KDKA was the first commercial radio station, but its fame derives from it being the first to broadcast presidential election returns.)

Santa Barbara

"My ranch may not be heaven, but it's got the same ZIP code." — Ronald Reagan on his Santa Barbara spread, quoted in the February 1999 *George*

"If you stayed here very long, you would probably cease to write anything, because you would cease to think—it is necessary out here and the natives regard it as morbid." —literary critic Edmund Wilson

"The ocean was inky; cool fog still wreathed the jacaranda. America's Riviera, the place actually made Olivia physically ill. The town seemed so pleased with itself, so appallingly unfazed by its own wealth. She had never seen so many frozen-yogurt shops in her life; everyone in town was fixated on putting friendly bacteria into their lower intestines. They were health know-it-alls, they knew the best foods, the best waters; they seemed perfectly content to outlive the poor." —from Scott Spencer's novel *Men in Black* (not the source of the Tommy Lee Jones-Will Smith movie)

"If, a thousand years from now, archaeologists happen to dig beneath the sands of Guadalupe, I hope that they will not rush into print with the amazing news that Egyptian civilization, far from being confined to the Valley of the Nile, extended all the way to the Pacific Coast of North America." —from the autobiography of film director Cecil B. De Mille; when shooting his 1926 film *The Ten Commandments* was completed in nearby Guadalupe, he ordered the sets buried in order to prevent any other film company from using them.

Colorado

Quips & Quirks

From the Internet: You Live in Colorado When…
You carry your $3,000 mountain bike atop your $500 car.
You tell your husband to pick up Granola on his way home and he stops at the day care center.
A pass does not involve a football or dating.
The top of your head is bald, but you still have a pony tail.

Cripple Creek

Lotta Nuggets—An 1891 gold rush in Cripple Creek near Pike's Peak eventually turned up more than $500 million worth of gold.

Denver

"Its new airport, with its dazzling white tent domes, can be a little disorienting when one comes to it from the plains to the east—is that Denver we're approaching or is it Mecca?" —author Larry McMurtry, *Roads: Driving America's Great Highways*

"Nestled up against the magnificent Rocky Mountains, Denver is the perfect destination for anyone who has trouble choosing between big-city and backwoods attractions or thinks a hard day's hell raising is best finished off with high tea at a 19th-century society hotel." —*www.lonelyplanet.com*

Inspired By The Rockies—The ice cream soda was invented in Denver.

Loveland Pass

"These high passes give you an eerie feeling. Because you come up out of summer heat and green vegetation and worldliness, and suddenly you're driving along in another world, a world of vast treeless sweeps, and queer roadside marshes that seem out of place, and cold little lakes and pools, and splotches of snow, and there's an indescribable kind of chill in the air, even though it's summer and the sun is hot." —journalist Ernie Pyle, June 20, 1939

Connecticut

Quips & Quirks

Am I Blue—The laws regulating conduct in 1781 Connecticut were printed on blue paper; hence the name "blue laws."

Bridgeport

"Bridgeport has not forgotten that, but for Barnum's efforts, the city might have been little more than a wide place in the road." —*Connecticut: A Guide to its Roads, Lore and People,* Federal Writers' Project, 1938; Barnum campaigned for federal funds to dredge Bridgeport's harbor, improve railroad service, and install a better water system.

Hartford

"I know of no lovelier country than that soft, sweeping woodsy land between Long Island Sound and Hartford. It is not spectacular country. But it's a little more than gently rolling, so that you get a long view when you top a rise, and it is so green and mapled and shaded and quiet—you get a feeling that the country has character, like a person. You can think of yourself as having sat down under a tree in Connecticut three hundred years ago and still be sitting there, growing mellow with the land, and you the winner and time the loser, because time had to pass on and you're still there in Connecticut." —journalist Ernie Pyle, August 16, 1935

Risky Business—The insurance industry, Hartford's mainstay, dates to February 8, 1794, when the Hartford Fire Insurance company issued its first policy (though the present company, known as The Hartford, wasn't established until 1810).

Aim High—Samuel Colt moved his company, Colt's Patent Fire Arms Manufacturing, from Paterson, N.J., to Hartford in 1855. Among his employees who gained a keen sense of modern manufacturing were Francis A. Pratt and Amos Whitney, who together founded an aircraft-engine manufacturing firm.

Litchfield

Thanks for Nothing—The first law school in America was founded in Litchfield in 1784.

Meriden

Beginnings—The world's first player piano was manufactured in Meriden in 1895.

Naugatauk

Some People Feel Like a Nut There—The Peter Paul candy plant in Naugatauk is the only place in the world where Mounds and Almond Joy candy bars are made.

Beginnings—Charles Goodyear perfected the process of vulcanizing rubber in Naugatauk in 1847.

New Britain

"The daughter of Berlin and the granddaughter of Farmington." —an appellation of the city based on where its founders had originated

New Haven

"A pork-packing plant on Long Wharf Road sometimes offends the passer-by with odors hardly less unpleasant than those formerly rising from the holds of the town's sealing ships, in from Patagonia, where in the early nineteenth century they sun-dried sealskins on a tract of land called 'the New Haven green.'" —*Connecticut: A Guide to its Roads, Lore and People,* Federal Writers' Project, 1938

And Yet They're Rivals—Yale was established in 1701 by several Connecticut clergymen, all of whom were graduates of Harvard. Graduates of Yale include patriot Nathan Hale, inventor Eli Whitney, vice-president John C. Calhoun, inventor Samuel F.B. Morse, presidential candidate Samuel Tilden, and president and chief justice William Howard Taft. Author James Fenimore Cooper was expelled in 1805.

Stonington

"Stonington and all its vicinity suffers in religion from the nearness of Rhode Island." —*Travels in New England and New York*

Delaware

Quips & Quirks

"Delaware is actually a state. You probably thought it was a suburb of Philadelphia, which isn't entirely incorrect." —*San Jose Mercury News columnist Mike Cassidy in an April 23, 2002, column entitled "Welcome to Delaware: It's small, but a great place to sue somebody."*

"Delaware has always been the Liechtenstein of America, a postage stamp of a state (100 miles long) with a minuscule population (780,000) but a critical role to play in the running of the American economy: More than 300,000 companies and 200,000 other business entities take advantage of the state's favorable laws and taxes and choose to be incorporated there." — Nicholas Varchaver, in the May 13, 2002, issue of *Fortune*

Wilmington

"Although it would take 80 Delawares to fill up all the Golden State, Delaware, much like Silicon Valley, has a healthy, some might say overblown, sense of its greatness. Where Silicon Valley defines its power in terms of being the world's technology capital, Delaware has come to expect that all of corporate America will come to its living room to resolve its feuds." —*San Jose Mercury News reporter Michelle Quinn, in Wilmington covering Walter Hewlett's suit to block Hewlett-Packard's acquisition of Compaq*

District of Columbia

Quips & Quirks

"Another city that gets a bad rap, largely because it is being jointly run by a city government on the cartoon side of inept and a Congress that hates it. It has become a kind of poster child for the ills of the modern welfare state. Still, it is a city of gracious neighborhoods, great museums, awe-inspiring historical sights, wonderful music, decent theater and not bad restaurants. It's a company town but, what the heck, it's our company." — syndicated columnist Donald Kaul

"Washington, D.C., is full of people who think that if they don't do their job, the world will stop." —Robert Reich, Clinton Administration Secretary of Labor

"At century's end, with Washington's follies on 24-hour display, it is difficult to recall that the city once seemed impossibly inaccessible, a marbled world where lawmakers all talked like Daniel Webster. But Cold War Washington did seem that way, and it was [Allen] Drury's fiction [in *Advise and Consent*] that brought the place to vivid life, using a confirmation battle to explore dark corners of ambition, sex, blackmail, and, in the end, statesmanship." —Jon Meacham in the January/February 1999 issue of *Stanford*

"There must be more world-savers and civilization-retrievers in Washington than in any city in the world." —journalist Ernie Pyle, November 15, 1940

"Outside of the killings, [Washington] has one of the lowest crime rates in the country." —Mayor Marion Barry

"The last time I cooperated with the *Washington Post* was in 1952, when I was a paper boy delivering the damn thing in northwest Washington." — commentator Patrick Buchanan, insisting that he was not Bob Woodward's Watergate source known as Deep Throat

"A person without competitiveness has little chance in Washington, D.C., whose elite echelons—journalistic, legal, bureaucratic—comprise one of the most competitive social entities on earth." —author Larry McMurtry, *Roads: Driving America's Great Highways*

"The Beltway protects our governing body from whatever chance infection of common sense might occasionally waft in from the country at large." —author Larry McMurtry, *Roads: Driving America's Great Highways*

"That city's divided on almost every issue. You can divide over Republican, Democrat. You have poverty. You have the rich. You have almost every cross section, and the only thing that unites the entire city is the Redskins. I once had an Iranian cab driver pick me up. The guy can't even find my house, but he's gotta tell me two weeks into the season to change quarterbacks." —Joe Gibbs, former head coach of the Washington Redskins, quoted in the September 1997 *George* in an article on Jack Kent Cooke

"Washington, on the edge of the real South, naturally has some of the South's delightful slothfulness... A good part of its population is in comfortable circumstances, so that the pinched look and the anxious stare and the goad of hurry, hurry, hurry settles but seldom on the citizens of Washington. The whole thing, summed up, makes for easy living. The New Deal, it is true, has brought a new alertness to Washington, and people with responsibility on their faces do rush about, but they seem to rush sort of slowly, in tune with the character of the city." —journalist Ernie Pyle, October 2, 1935

"If you want a friend in Washington, get a dog." —Harry S. Truman, 33rd president of the United States

"Washington is the kind of place where people seriously discuss whether Socks, the presidential cat, will write a book. It all seems to be about how close you are to the throne. It's like those fish in the Amazon who get really powerful and huge and swell up and turn beautiful colors. Those are the people who are close to the President, and you can tell instantly who they are when you're in Washington." —Diana McLellan, former gossip columnist for the *Washington Post*

"All the world is a high school, and after graduation, the student-council presidents go to Washington and the class wits go to New York." —author Michele Slung (who divides her time between both cities)

"I have frequently had conversations where the New Yorker is talking nonstop, and I can see that the Washingtonian is waiting for the right moment to come in. But the New Yorker doesn't pause long enough to let

them. They think the other person has nothing to say and just keeps going."
—linguist Dr. Deborah Tannen

"There's enough fat in the government in Washington that if it was rendered and made into soap, it would wash the world." —Ronald Reagan

"It is sometimes called the City of Magnificent Distances, but it might with greater propriety be termed the City of Magnificent Intentions; for it is only on taking a bird's-eye view of it from the top of the Capitol that one can at all comprehend the vast designs of its projector, an aspiring Frenchman. Spacious avenues that begin in nothing, and lead nowhere; streets, mile long, that only want houses, roads, and inhabitants; public buildings that need but a public to be complete; and ornaments of great thoroughfares, which only lack great thoroughfares to ornament—are its leading features." —author Charles Dickens during his 1842 visit

"The green esplanade that extends to the obelisk erected in memory of George Washington is more disheartening than the Champ-de-Mars. Despite the soft light and the freshness of the grass, it looks to me like a torrid desert—boredom burns. In the whiteness of their marble, the museums and embassies refract the dull heat of a relentless summer." —philosopher Simone de Beauvoir, February 14, 1947

"Its tree-lined avenues and grand 19th-century buildings create a surprisingly warm, almost cozy atmosphere—though some neighborhoods are less so than others. The capital is a microcosm of the grand ideals and grim realities of the US—as the potholes and homeless people everywhere will attest." —*www.lonelyplanet.com*

Endings—Woodrow Wilson left the White House in 1921, but instead of going back to New Jersey, where he had been president of Princeton University and governor of the state, he moved to 2340 S St. NW in Washington, D.C., where he died three years later (the only president besides Lincoln to actually die in Washington). The building is preserved today as a museum—the only presidential museum in the city.

Florida

Quips & Quirks

"Where the earth meets the water, and forms mud." —proposed state motto from humorist Dave Barry

"If it wasn't for Florida, I'd be quite a rich man today." —Henry M. Flagler, who invested in both St. Augustine and Key West

From the Internet: You Live in Florida When...
- You eat dinner at 3:15 in the afternoon.
- All purchases include a coupon of some kind, even houses and cars.
- Everyone can recommend an excellent dermatologist.
- Road construction never ends anywhere in the state.
- Cars in front of you are often driven by headless people.
- There are only giant doctors because every person's doctor is "the Biggest" in his field

Daytona Beach

"This place is so cheesy. It's just a living hell. Drinking is the only way to survive the pure cheesiness." —Ivan Gaviria, a visiting Duke University student, quoted in the March 27, 1989, *St. Petersburg Times*

Fort Lauderdale

"As recently as the late 1980s, the sand in Fort Lauderdale was sticky with beer and the streets ran wild with pimpled youths storming about in celebration of that American university rite of passage, Spring Break. Locals would look on in horror as their city was overtaken by yahoos, and they finally decided to do something about it. They renovated, groomed and trimmed the whole place, turning Fort Lauderdale into more of an international yachting center than an intercollegiate multi-kegger." — *www.lonelyplanet.com*

Gainesville

It's A Silly Name Otherwise—Back in 1965, during football practice, University of Florida football players were becoming dehydrated in the Florida heat. The coaches asked university doctors what they could do, and in response, the doctors devised a drink for the players that contained both electrolytes and carbohydrates. The restorative drink took the name of the team, and that's why it's called Gatorade.

Jacksonville

Largest City in Land Area—At 840 square miles, Jacksonville is the largest city in the mainland U.S.

Key West

"This faraway little city is going through one interesting transition. It doesn't know whether it is going to become another Palm Beach, a Coney Island, or a public charge [welfare recipient], or just stay the way it always was. And worst of all, it doesn't know which of these it *wants* to become." —journalist Ernie Pyle, January 23, 1939

"See the Lower Keys on your hands and knees was our old advertising slogan—a tragic admission that outside of watching the sun sink behind the mangrove islands and the ospreys drift lazily across the azure sky, there wasn't a whole lot to do down here except drive until you heave." —Barbara Ehrenreich in *Time*

"The Florida Keys, modest pods of earth protruding from a great sea, with U.S. 1 superimposed upon them, would certainly seem to validate my theory that littorals produce a gentle but distinctive seediness." —author Larry McMurtry, *Roads: Driving America's Great Highways*

"If you insist on living in a hot, humid atmosphere enlivened by terrifying insects, you can't do better than this. It is a loose, funky place where you are allowed to name your own poison, then sip it. It makes New Orleans seem like a military school." —syndicated columnist Donald Kau

"This is a tolerant place, usually. Greasy bikers in black leather and mirrored shades cruise their rumbling Harley-Davidsons down streets filled with college boys on pastel scooters... It is a mantra here: Live and let live. There is room, even on an island just two miles long and four miles wide, for everyone and everything." —*New York Times* reporter Rick Bragg

"It looked like something in a dream." —author John Dos Passos, in a letter to Ernest Hemingway

"I hear they're buying up lots, and then after the poor people are starved out and gone somewhere else to starve some more they're going to come in and make it into a beauty spot for tourists." —Harry Morgan, the hero of Hemingway's *To Have and Have Not*

Yankees In Florida—Because a group of soldiers acted quickly to take control of nearby Fort Taylor on the day that Florida seceded from the U.S., Key West was the only city south of the Mason-Dixon line to be held by Union forces for the entire Civil War.

Hard to Believe—In 1880, Key West was the largest city in Florida.

Miami

"This is Dade County. If it's going to get weird, it's going to get weird here." —Metro-Dade police spokeswoman Linda O'Brien, when divers initially found little wreckage from ValuJet 592's crash site in the Everglades, May 1996

"Orlando, thanks to Disney and the space center, is now the Capitol of Clean, the place where families go, whereas Miami, which David Rieff has called the capital of Latin America, is the place where swingers go, where the music is loud, sexual peculiarities tolerated, and drugs plentiful." —author Larry McMurtry, *Roads: Driving America's Great Highways*

"It used to be called 'God's Waiting Room.' And even today, if you mention Miami to someone who hasn't been here or read about it lately, they might conjure up a blurry memory of octogenarians mingling poolside while Aunt Sadie implored them to wait half an hour after eating before going into the water." —*www.lonelyplanet.com*

"Puggy liked everything about Miami. He liked that it was warm. He liked that most of the police seemed tolerant of people like him—people who, merely by existing, tended to violate laws that solid citizens never even thought about, like how long you were allowed to sit in a certain place without buying something. The attitude of most of the police down here seemed to be, hey, you can *sit* all you want; we're just glad you're not *shooting*." —from *Miami Herald* columnist Dave Barry's *Big Trouble*

"*Big Trouble* is outrageously warped, cheerfully depraved—and harrowingly close to true life in Florida. This book will do for our tourism industry what Dennis Rodman did for bridal wear." —Florida author Carl Hiaasen

Orlando

"Orlando is a pretty moral town. If God was going to hurl a meteor… you'd think he'd start with Las Vegas." —Orlando minister Randy Young

"Orlando is the only large or largish city not set on a beach, unless you count Gainesville, which essentially is just a college." —author Larry McMurtry, *Roads: Driving America's Great Highways*

"Before Orlando became an extension of Disney Corp.'s expansionist dreams, it was known as the 'city built on the peel of an orange.' In other words, citrus was at the turn of the century what mouse ears are today. The citrus boom straddled railroad and real estate booms, but none of these compare to the well-honed tourist boom in full swing today." —*www.lonelyplanet.com*

St. Petersburg
"I'm writing you from the home of the newly wed and the nearly dead." —letter from Sara Lessley, a newly hired *St. Petersburg Times* reporter, 1980

Beginnings—In 1918, St. Petersburg was the first city to hire its own public relations person.

Tampa
"I'm all for it." —John McKay, first coach of the Tampa Bay Buccaneers (2-14 in 1976, its first season), when asked what he thought of his team's execution

Ybor City
"Worn-out brick buildings cling to old wrought-iron porch rails and latticework. The street corner air is thick with the aroma of coffee and tobacco, the side streets dotted with historic inns and clubs. Buy a cigar here and it comes with history, and likely from a grandson of the original makers." —Steven Girardi, writing in the summer 2001 *Smoke*

Georgia

Quips & Quirks

Biggest in the East—Georgia is the largest state east of the Mississippi.

What Australia Owes Georgia—Originally, Georgia was England's penal colony in the New World. When the colonists won the Revolutionary War, England was forced to find a new penal colony—which led to the colonization of Australia.

Atlanta

"The city seems...both Southern and Northern, global and provincial, black run and white dominated—a liberal conservative small town done up in a three-piece suit. The two phrases most closely associated with Atlanta are, after all, "I have a dream," and "Frankly my dear, I don't give a damn." The riddle at the heart of Atlanta has always been how to balance the bright new equality envisaged by the Rev. Martin Luther King Jr. with the "don't-give-a-damn" romance of the Old South immortalized by Margaret Mitchell." —Pico Iyer, in *Time's* summer 1996 special issue on the Olympics

"This is the metropolis...whose mayor once toyed with the idea of renaming city streets and parks after commercial sponsors, painting corporate logos on city garbage trucks and implanting ads in city sidewalks." —Newspaper Enterprise Association writer Joseph Spear in an October 5, 1997, *San Jose Mercury-News* article decrying the municipal sale of advertising space

"The city has also suffered from overzealous college get-downs and from the relentless development that's razed much of what it hasn't converted to shopping malls. But there are offbeat neighborhoods to explore and old-fashioned towns nearby where you can still savor something of bygone days." —*www.lonelyplanet.com*

"To these black college students shaking it in front of his Lexus, this was nothing more than what white college students had been doing for years at Fort Lauderdale and Daytona and Cancún, or wherever they were going now, except that these boys and girls here in front of him weren't interested in the beach. They were coming to the...streets of Atlanta. Atlanta, the Black Beacon, as the Mayor called it, 70 percent black... White Atlanta was screaming its head off about 'Freaknik,' with a k instead of a c, as the white newspapers called it, ignorant of the fact that Freaknik was a variation not of the (white) word beatnik but of the (neutral) word *picnic*." —from Tom Wolfe's *A Man in Full*

Endings—On Peachtree Street in Atlanta on August 16, 1949, *Gone with the Wind* author Margaret Mitchell was stuck and killed by a car.

Savannah

"Savannah is sleeping amid its baskets of azaleas. From north to south, from east to west, the city consists of peaceful squares connected by flowering lanes. Each square is surrounded by old dwellings, sometimes with a colonial church rising in their midst. In the middle of the square there's a large bed planted with azaleas, which are beginning to unfurl their leaves, and in the center of the flowerbed there's a tarnished bronze statue: some general or hero from the Revolutionary War or Civil War." —philosopher Simone de Beauvoir, April 3, 1947

"Locals are mixed in their reaction to [what they call] 'the Book' [John Behrendt's *Midnight in the Garden of Good and Evil*]. They are keenly aware that it has had a major impact on tourism, that it has brought wealth and fame to their once-sleepy Southern town. But they don't care to be thought of as a slightly deviant bouquet of exotic hothouse blooms whose closets are crammed with any number of skeletons." —travel writer Diana C. Gleasner, writing in the February 24, 2002, *Buffalo News*

First Planned City—Founder James Oglethorpe laid out Savannah in a series of grids that allowed for wide streets and public squares; of his original 24 squares, 21 remain.

Hawaii

Quips & Quirks

"Why did not Captain Cook have taste enough to call his great discovery the Rainbow Islands? These charming spectacles are present to you at every turn; they are common in all the Islands; they are visible every day, and frequently at night also—not the silvery bow we see once in an age in the States, by moonlight, but barred with all bright and beautiful colors, like the children of the sun and rain. I saw one of them a few nights ago. What the sailors call "rain-dogs"—little patches of rainbow—are often seen drifting about the heavens in these latitudes, like stained cathedral windows." —Mark Twain in *Roughing It*

"No other land could longingly and so beseechingly haunt me, sleeping and waking, through half a lifetime." —Mark Twain

"You get up every day, and no matter how bad things are, it's a beautiful day. And the worst of Hawaii is so much better than where [constituents] came from. Politicians take advantage of people's good nature." —gubernatorial candidate Linda Lingle, speaking to columnist George Will about the challenge of changing the status quo in paradise, 2002

It's So Tasty Too—At 4.3 million cans per year, Hawaii leads the U.S. in consumption of Spam.

Hana

"There is nothing quite comparable when you think of waterfalls, natural swimming pools, and the ocean beyond." —aviator Charles Lindbergh, who is buried in a small churchyard in Kipahulu on the Hana Highway

Hawaii (The Big Island)

"One could stand on that mountain (wrapped up in blankets and furs to keep warm), and while he nibbled a snow-ball or an icicle to quench his thirst he could look down the long sweep of its sides and see spots where plants are growing that grow only where the bitter cold of winter prevails; lower down he could see sections devoted to productions that thrive in the temperate zone alone; and at the bottom of the mountain he could see the home of the tufted cocoa-palms and other species of vegetation that grow only in the sultry atmosphere of eternal summer. He could see all the climes of the world at a single glance of the eye, and that glance would only pass over a distance of four or five miles as the bird flies!" —Mark Twain on Mauna Loa, from *Roughing It*

"You cannot take anything, including yourself, too seriously for very long in Hawaii... So I think the presidential candidates should have to spend the campaign in Hawaii, alone, without their pollsters and their wingtipped entourages... Under those conditions, maybe even the candidates—even those frantic, twitching, driven men—would eventually mellow out. Maybe one day, lying on the beach, they'd announce: "Hey, I can't remember my economic program!" —Dave Barry, "Rummy Idea to Put Politicos In Proper Place." September 22, 1996

Lahaina

"One of the breathing holes of hell...a sight to make a missionary weep." —anonymous minister, 1846

Honolulu

"Honolulu doesn't seem like a military or naval city, in the sense that San Diego is a Navy city. Soldiers and sailors are all about, yet the military doesn't seem to dominate. I guess maybe it's just lost in the constantly passing scene of strange races, big businesses, steamships, sugar, beauty, vacationists, and Hawaiian lore that make up the personality of Honolulu." —journalist Ernie Pyle, January 27, 1938

Beginnings—Actress Nicole Kidman was born in Honolulu on June 20, 1967; her father, an Australian Navy officer, was stationed there as a liaison to the U.S. Navy.

Idaho

Quips & Quirks

"In no state is there such obvious hatred of law and government—hard to explain, since there is scant evidence that there *is* much law and government in Idaho. A lot of frontier types who are quite up to Alaska hang out there." —author Larry McMurtry, *Roads: Driving America's Great Highways*

Coeur d'Alene
"The saying is, 'relax, you're in northern Idaho now.' You don't have to honk your horn or wear makeup every day." —resident Carrie Chase, quoted in "The 10 Best Places To Live," July 1996 *Swing*

Sun Valley
"It contains more delightful features for a winter sports center than any other place I have seen in the United States, Switzerland, or Austria." — Count Felix Schaffgotsch, in a 1935 telegram to railroad tycoon Averell Harriman, who built a ski resort there to boost ridership on the Union Pacific

"We don't put up with that from anybody. Everybody here has some money. Celebrities are treated like everyone else." —a longtime resident commenting on the fact that celebrities like Clint Eastwood and Arnold Schwarzenegger are not allowed to cut in line at restaurants

"Our local mantra used to be: we don't know, we don't see, we don't tell. We did well by the celebrities and in return we protected their privacy. It was an unspoken but widely practiced code of silence. This experience has shaken our notions of how we behave around them." —Hailey lawyer E. Lee Schender, quoted by Andrew Gumbel in a November 14, 1999, *London Independent* story about the effect on the town when actor Bruce Willis abruptly closed the restaurants he owned there and cancelled all other investments

Endings—On July 2, 1961, in the valley town of Ketchum, Ernest Hemingway died of a shotgun blast. Some friends believed he committed suicide; his wife insisted it was a gun-cleaning accident.

Illinois

Quips & Quirks

The Name's the Same—Because of the Mississippi's resemblance to the Nile, you'll find towns in southern Illinois named Cairo, Thebes, Karnak, and Dongola.

Chicago

"I miss everything about Chicago except January and February." —actor Gary Cole

"It has a long stupid face and looks like some giant insect that is about to eat a smaller, weaker insect. It has eyes that are pitiless, cold, mean. But why not? Everybody said it had the spirit of Chicago. And from thousands of miles away, accidentally or on purpose, Picasso captured it. Up there in that ugly face is the spirit of Al Capone, the Summerdale scandal cops, the settlers who took the Indians but good. Its eyes are like the eyes of every slum owner who made a buck off the small and weak. And of every building inspector who took a wad from a slum owner to make it all possible. It has the look of the dope pusher and of the syndicate technician as he looks for just the right wire to splice the bomb to... Picasso has never been here, they say. You'd think he's been riding the L all his life." —from Mike Royko's August 16, 1967, *Tribune* column after the unveiling of the Picasso sculpture in Civic Center Plaza.

"From north to south, east to west, the streets are crossed and inhabited by the metallic architecture of the elevated railroad, familiarly known by the El. This iron ceiling transforms the avenues into dark tunnels; beams shaken by the passing trains fill the air with groans that penetrate the houses; it's a great natural voice, like the wind in the forests." —Author Simone de Beauvoir, May 11, 1947

"I love this town, but I can't stand the weather. I remember the first time it got below zero with snow on the ground and I said, 'We're going to go out and play football in *that?*'" —California native and former Chicago Bears tight end Ryan Wetnight

"[My father-in-law] used to say, 'If you can't make a living in Chicago, you can't make a living anywhere.' They don't care here where you've come from, as long as you're honest and work hard." —Jerry Reinsdorf, owner of the Chicago Bulls and White Sox, quoted in June 30, 1997, *Sports Illustrated*

"In seasons when the Cubs or Bears are out of it early, I spend a lot of time cleaning my garage. I'm worried that my garage, by the end of summer, will be spotless. I might even repaint it." —comedian Bill Murray, quoted in the June 10, 2002, *Sports Illustrated*

"This is Chicago. Anything can happen." —Studs Terkel in *Eight Men Out*

"On a cold, brutally windy day in Chicago, when the temperature's sub-zero and strong gusts keep you from walking down the street, the first question that will come to mind is, 'Who the hell decided to build a city and settle here?'" —*www.lonelyplanet.com*

"Chicago got started when a bunch of people in New York said, 'Gee, I'm enjoying the crime and the poverty, but it just isn't cold enough. Let's go west.'" —comedian Richard Jeni

"It was like a Catholic school kid going over to the publics. It was like ordering a Chicago-style dog with sauerkraut. It was like handing a cop a brown bag with not so much as a dollar in it. It was something that in Chicago simply was not done." —journalist Mike Cassidy reminiscing about announcer Harry Carey switching from the White Sox to the Cubs

Gangster Gunned Down—After seeing the Clark Gable film *Manhattan Melodrama* with the legendary "lady in red" who fingered him, John Dillinger was gunned down outside the Biograph Theater at 2433 N. Lincoln Ave. in Chicago on July 22, 1934.

Collision Damage Waiver Not Included—In 1922, a man named Walter L. Jacobs began renting Ford Model Ts in Chicago, the first time anyone had rented cars. The following year, Jacobs sold his business to a man named John Hertz (who'd also founded the Yellow Cab Co. in New York).

City of Big Conventions —More political conventions have been held in Chicago than any other city—25 between 1860 and 1996.

First Department Store—In 1852, Marshall Field of Chicago was the first entrepreneur to sell different kinds of merchandise under one roof.

Decatur

"It's just another setback in the life of the armpit of Illinois." —resident Jeff Senger on the closure of the Bridgestone/Firestone plant in June, 2001

Waukegan

Beginnings—Both comedian Jack Benny and science fiction writer Ray Bradbury were born in Waukegan.

Indiana

Quips & Quirks

"In northern Indiana, especially Gary, people seemed worried about the prospects of being taken over by Chicago. In the south, they were threatened by Kentucky, in the west, by Illinois, and in the east, by Ohio. It was as though in Indiana they have to think Indiana for fear that if they do not, it will be absorbed by the outside world." —former Minnesota senator Eugene McCarthy

Bloomfield

Population Center—In the 1890 census, the population center of the U.S. was just outside Unionville. In the 2000 census, the population center of the U.S. was Bloomfield.

Dana

"Dana is a pretty town. Nearly every street is just a cool, dark tunnel, formed by the great arching maple trees on either side." —journalist Ernie Pyle on his home town

Evansville

"Evansville is a link between the unhurried Old South and the bustling, industrial north... For many years it was a vital link between Northern farmers and the markets of the south, and even now the impressive volume of its river freight and its busy water front give Evansville the characteristic atmosphere of a river town." —from the Works Progress Administration's 1938 *Indiana, A Guide to the Hoosier State*

Fort Wayne

Beginnings—What may have been the first night baseball game was played at the foot of Calhoun St. in Fort Wayne between a team of pros from Quincy, Illinois, and a team of students from the Fort Wayne Episcopal College. The electric lights were set up by the Fort Wayne Jenney Electric Light Company, a predecessor of General Electric.

Indianapolis

"The visitor's first impression is one of spacious friendliness—broad streets, an almost Southern leisureliness, and fewer tall buildings than are seen in most cities of comparable size... Built on level ground with plenty of room to expand, the city was patterned after Washington, D.C. Its streets intersect at right angles and four great avenues cut away from the business section." —from the Works Progress Administration's 1938 *Indiana, A Guide to the Hoosier State*

Strike That—Charles H. Black built what may be the first automobile with an internal combustion engine in Indianapolis in 1891, but he used a kerosene torch for the ignition, which would blow out on windy days and was quickly deemed impractical; other automotive firsts for Indianapolis include four-wheel brakes and the six-cylinder engine. The first Indianapolis 500 race in 1911 was won by a Marmon, a locally manufactured car.

Endings—Benjamin Harrison, 23rd president and grandson of 9th president William Henry Harrison, died in Indianapolis on March 13, 1901; he lived for many years at 1230 N. Delaware St. and was buried in Crown Hill Cemetery at 3402 Boulevard Place. Two vice-presidents (Charles W. Fairbanks and Thomas R. Marshall) are there as well, as is Indiana poet James Whitcomb Riley.

Last Concert—Elvis Presley gave his last concert at Indianapolis' Market Square Arena in 1977; the Arena itself was imploded in July of 2001.

Muncie

"The Lynds [sociologists Robert and Helen] might have chosen Kokomo, Anderson, Marion, Peoria, Walla Walla, or any other of a hundred average American towns for their study [*Middletown*, 1929]; they chose Muncie not because it was exceptional but because it was thoroughly typical and had certain characteristics that made it more suitable for their purposes than any other small city." —from the Works Progress Administration's 1938 *Indiana, A Guide to the Hoosier State*

New Harmony

"In spite of its placid present, New Harmony belongs to the world-aristocracy of villages that have made history. Students of cultural evolution and social reform remember it as the scene of two notable efforts to build a perfect communal society. The forests were cleared, the soil was cultivated, and the first sturdy buildings were erected by the Rappites, an ascetic religious group that came from Germany to Pennsylvania in 1805 and in 1815 founded the village of Harmonie on the Wabash. Then in 1824 the Rappites sold their village to Robert Owen, Scotch philanthropist, industrialist, and social reformer, who attempted here in New Harmony, as he called it, to found a new social order, a communal mode of living that was expected to eradicate the evils of exploitation, poverty, and competition." — from the Works Progress Administration's 1938 *Indiana, A Guide to the Hoosier State*

South Bend

Whatever Happened to?—The Studebaker car company was founded in South Bend by Clement and Henry Studebaker, brothers who like their father John originally manufactured wagons.

Endings—Legendary Notre Dame football coach Knute Rockne is buried in Highland Cemetery on Portage Avenue in South Bend.

Iowa

Quips & Quirks

"Being rude and killing someone are about on par here." —Roxanne Conlin, 1982 Democratic nominee for governor

Davenport

Isn't It Ironic?—In one of life's odd twists, London-born Cary Grant, the personification of suave and debonair for three decades of Hollywood, died in Davenport, America's agricultural heartland, on November 29, 1986, suffering a stroke just before giving one of his famous question-and-answer presentations.

Des Moines

"There were beautiful bevies of girls everywhere I looked in Des Moines that afternoon—they were coming home from high school—but I had no time now for thoughts like that and promised myself a ball in Denver... So I rushed past the pretty girls, and the prettiest girls in the world live in Des Moines." —from Jack Kerouac's *On The Road*

Mason City

"Mason City has two seasons: winter and August." —DJ Ray Arthur

West Branch

Beginnings—31st president Herbert Hoover was born in West Branch on August 10, 1874, the first president born in Iowa and the first born west of the Mississippi.

Kansas

Quips & Quirks

"There is a saying here that freaks are raised for export only. In one sense the saying is true enough, for what strikes one particularly is that, on the whole, native Kansans are all so much alike. It is a community of great solidarity, and to the native it is 'the Easterner' who appears eccentric." — from Carl Becker's 1910 book *Kansas*

"You might truthfully say there is nothing left of western Kansas. As far as the eye could see, there was nothing. There was not a tree, or a blade of grass, or a dog or a cow, or a human being—nothing whatever, nothing at all but gray raw earth and a few far houses and barns, sticking up from the dark gray sea like white cattle skeletons on the desert. There was nobody in the houses. The humans had given up, and gone. It was death, if I have ever seen death." —journalist Ernie Pyle, May 7, 1938

"Today, Kansas, born from radical conflict, is a state first to back a war and last to join a revolution, a place once wobbling almost to toppling but now become a land of equipoise, a seeming still point at the center of a revolving nation, a state where movements end rather than begin." —from William Least Heat Moon's *Prairy Erth*

"They call Kansas the 'Sunflower State,' not because it is overrun with the noxious weed, but because, as the sunflower turns on its stem to catch the first beams of the morning sun, and with its bread disk and yellow rays follows the great orb of the day, so Kansas turns to catch the first rays of every advancing thought or civilized agency, and with her broad prairies and gold fields welcomes and follows the light." —from an 1887 editorial in the *Burlington Nonpareil*

Blue Sky Laws—Kansas was the first state to enact laws against fraudulent stocks and bonds, so called because they promised nothing but blue sky. These laws were eventually became the basis for regulations enforced by the federal Securities and Exchange Commission.

Atchison

Named for a One-Day President—Best remembered today as part of the song, "On The Atchison, Topeka, and the Santa Fe," the town of Atchison was ironically named for a slavery-advocating senator from

Missouri named David Atchison. Atchison is also known in the annals of political trivia as the man who was president for a single day. Because March 4, 1849, was a Sunday, Zachary Taylor did not take the oath of office until Monday, March 5th. But James Polk's term of office officially ended at noon that Sunday, and his vice-president, George Mifflin Dallas (for whom the city of Dallas is named), had already resigned the previous Friday. Following Dallas' resignation, the other senator from Missouri, Thomas Hart Benton, nominated Atchison to be president pro tempore of the Senate, and he was elected. Following the strict guidelines of Article II of the constitution, Atchison was indeed president from noon on Sunday the 4th until the moment Taylor recited the presidential oath on Monday the 5th.

Cottonwood Falls

"A grizzled country of narrow, fertile lowlands and wide, depressing uplands, which smiles a few days in the spring and relapses into sullenness during the remainder of the year; a country with cattle on a thousand low-flung and menacing hills and the green and purple of alfalfa in the threads between." —Jay E. House, Philadelphia newspaper columnist, writing about the country near Cottonwood Falls where Notre Dame coach Knute Rockne—famous for inventing the forward pass—was killed in a plane crash on March 31, 1931. (Rockne was on his way to Hollywood to appear in a talking picture; because it was determined that a rotten wooden wing caused the crash, within two years, TWA and United Airlines both contracted to buy newly designed metal planes with dual engines—respectively, the Douglas Aircraft DC-1 and Boeing 247.)

"The Flint Hills don't take your breath away—they give you a chance to catch it." —Jim Hoy, quoted in William Least Heat Moon's *Prairie Erth*

Dodge City

"In 1882, Dodge City took its turn as the cowboy capital of the Southwest and rode high on the wave of prosperity. Outfits of cattlemen jostled freighters, hunters and soldiers in the streets that echoed to ribald songs and yells of the cowboy, and the wild oaths of the bullwhacker and the muleskinner. The law was 100 miles away at Hays—a town not without high color of its own." —from *The WPA Guide to 1930s Kansas*

They Died With Their Boots On—A promontory of gypsum (currently at the intersection of 4th Avenue and Spruce St.) in Dodge City was used as a lookout spot above the Arkansas River Valley. Sometime in 1872, two nameless cowboys camped out on what was then a nameless hill.

After a gunfight between the two, the victor fled and the victim was covered with his blankets and buried with his boots on; forever after, it was known as Boot Hill (note: Fort Hays also lays claim to the first Boot Hill).

Fort Hays

"The town consists of shanties, dugouts, and tents; there are forty-two saloons, one hundred and ten harlots, crowds of gamblers, and all the noted desperadoes make their headquarters here." —*St. Louis Journal* reporter, 1867

Fort Scott

"Local tradition in Fort Scott asserts that the term 'Jayhawker' originated with the patrons of the Free State Hotel. Pat Devlin, an Irishman and a member of Captain [James] Montgomery's band, so the story goes, returned late one afternoon from plundering pro-slavery farmers along the Missouri-Kansas border. Asked where he had been he replied that he had been 'jayhawking.' 'The jayhawk,' he went onto explain, 'is a bird in Ireland that catches small birds and bullyrags the life out of them like cats do mice. I'm in the same business myself and I call it jayhawking.' Jayhawker was taken up by Captain Montgomery as a nickname for his band and finally stuck as a name for all Kansas." —from *The WPA Guide to 1930s Kansas*

Garden City

"If you would like to have your heart broken, just come out here. This is the dust-storm country. It is the saddest land I have ever seen. Coming in here from Colorado Springs, a one-day drive, you pass through both the sandstorm and the dust-storm regions. Eastern Colorado is a mild form of desert, and hence rather sandy. When the wind blows there, you have a sandstorm. As you get into Kansas, the soil becomes richer and softer, and when it gets dry and powdery, and when the wind blows, you have a dust storm." —journalist Ernie Pyle, June 6, 1936

Manhattan

Well, It Was Some City Back East—Before they agreed to change it to Manhattan, the first settlers of the town had named it Boston.

Medicine Lodge

The Hatchet Came Later—Prohibitionist Carry Nation first stormed a saloon in her home town of Medicine Lodge in the summer of 1899, brandishing her umbrella and insisting the proprietor would go to hell. It wasn't until late in 1900 that she brandished a hatchet at a saloon, this time in Wichita.

Russell

"Bob Dole hails from rural Kansas [Russell, just off I-70], where they put a star next to vanilla ice cream on the menu, denoting 'Hot and Spicy.'" —Jeff Greenfield writing in *Time* the week before the 1996 New York state primary, questioning how Dole and other candidates would survive the gauntlet of New York ethnic food

Topeka

Brown vs. Board of Education—On behalf of his daughter Linda, Oliver Brown sued the Topeka Board of Education in 1954 to enable her to attend the school closest to their house. Eventually, the case went to the Supreme Court, which used it to eliminate segregated schools.

Potato Town—One early settler wanted to name the town after Daniel Webster, but a local reverend suggested they use Topeka, an Omaha Indian word meaning "a good place to dig potatoes." The reverend's suggestion won out.

Kentucky

Quips & Quirks

"The state of Ohio is separated from Kentucky just by one river; on either side of it the soil is equally fertile, and the situation equally favorable, and yet everything is different. Here [Ohio is] a population devoured by feverish activity, trying every means to make its fortune; the population seems poor to look at, for they work with their hands, but that work is the source of riches. There [in Kentucky] are people who make others work for them and show little compassion, a people without energy, mettle or the spirit of enterprise. On one side of the stream, work is honored and leads to all else, on the other it is despised as the mark of servitude... These differences cannot be attributed to any other cause but slavery. It degrades the black population and enervates the white." —Alexis de Tocqueville, December 2, 1831

"In the parts of Kentucky and Tennessee through which we passed the men are big and strong; they have a national physiognomy, and an energetic look. By no means like the inhabitants of Ohio, who are a confused mass, a mixture of all the American races, they on the contrary all come from a common stock and belong to the great Virginian family. So, too, they have much more than any other Americans we have yet met, that instinctive love of country, a love mixed up with exaggeration and prejudices, and something entirely different from the reasoned feeling and the refined egotism which bears the name of patriotism in almost all the States of the Union." —Alexis de Tocqueville, December, 1831

They Started Out Together—Jefferson Davis, president of the Confederacy, was born in Fairview on June 8, 1808, just 100 miles from Hodgenville, where Abraham Lincoln was born eight months later on February 12, 1809 (Lincoln was the first president born outside the 13 colonies).

Bardstown

My Old Kentucky Home—Perhaps the only town in the South to celebrate a Yankee who never lived there, Bardstown commemorates songwriter Stephen Foster, who penned "My Old Kentucky Home" after an 1850s visit to Federal Hill, an estate in bluegrass country.

Harlan

"The murders that do occur in mountain counties like Harlan and Letcher often seem to occur while someone is in a drunken rage, and often among members of the same family—a father shooting a son over something trivial, one member of a family mowing down another who is breaking down the door trying to get at a third. 'We got people in this county today who would kill you as quick as look at you,' [attorney Daniel Boone] Smith has said. 'But most of 'em are the type that don't bother you if you leave them alone.'" —from 1971 book Calvin Trillin's *U.S. Journal*

Louisville

"There was nothing very interesting in the scenery of this day's journey, which brought us at midnight to Louisville. We slept at the Galt House; a splendid hotel; and were as handsomely lodged as though we had been in Paris, rather than hundreds of miles beyond the Alleghenies." —author Charles Dickens during his 1842 visit

Tug Fork Creek

Feud for Thought—You've probably never heard of Tug Fork Creek, which forms part of the Kentucky-West Virginia border, but you've heard of the people who lived there. Along this creek was the home of Randolph McCoy and his 13 children, one of whom allegedly shot one of William Anderson Hatfield's 13 children, who lived on the West Virginia side. Although the murder took place in 1882, there had been bad blood between the families in the past over stolen pigs and the fact that the Hatfields, even though they were in West Virginia, sided with the Confederacy, while the McCoys, even though they were in Kentucky, sided with the Union. Although most of the feuding between the Hatfields and the McCoys was over by 1888 (mostly because several were sent to jail), sporadic gun battles continued between members of the two families past the turn of the century.

Louisiana

Quips & Quirks

Atchafalaya Swamp

"[It's] a land of mystery that extends much of the way between Baton Rouge and Lafayette... If 'majestic' is a word that fits the Mississippi in its lower reaches, 'spooky' is a good word for the Atchafalaya. Except for the bird sounds, it is largely a silent world—the snakes and alligators and other water creatures that inhabit it make little noise." —author Larry McMurtry, *Roads: Driving America's Great Highways*

New Orleans

"The French of Louisiana are not enterprising in business; they do not at all like to risk what they have got on a chance, and they fear the disgrace of bankruptcy. The Americans who descend on us every year from the North are eaten up with longing for wealth; they have long given up everything else for that; they come with little to lose and very few of the honourable scruples the French feel about paying their debts." —the French Consul of New Orleans, quoted by Alexis de Tocqueville, January 1, 1832

"One comes upon New Orleans in the unlikeliest of places, by penetrating the depths of the Bible Belt, running the gauntlet of Klan territory, the pine barrens of south Mississippi, Bogalusa and the Florida parishes of Louisiana." —Southern author Walker Percy

"Through its storms, its sun, its humid nights, its pearl gray spring smelling of autumn, New Orleans seems worthy of its most fabulous legends. I know it's also one of the poorest cities in America, where life is extremely harsh; its stagnant luxury already seems ambiguous to us, and we would have liked to penetrate further into its heart, to live here in the reality of its daily life. On leaving, I resolve: 'I will return.'" —philosopher Simone de Beauvoir, April 2, 1947

"The unofficial state motto, *laissez les bons temps rouler* (let the good times roll), pretty much says it all for most people—and let there be no mistake, New Orleans rolls plenty." —*www.lonelyplanet.com*

"Mardi Gras used to be a special day. We waited for it and enjoyed it. Now we have it every day. Any convention or group that can afford it can stage a parade now. They roll all the time, people wander around in beads year round. We're becoming a caricature of ourselves." —Louis Sahuc, New Orleans photographer

"Almost no one in New Orleans runs because they actually like running. We run so we can eat and drink and party that much more." —banker Colleen McEvoy

"Will we ever meet again in Jackson Square at dawn to eat beignets and drink big mugs of hot, black coffee heavy with chicory and sleep?" —*Fortune* columnist Stanley Bing, bemoaning the recession's effect on convention travel, February 2, 2002

"New Orleans, a city where so many closets are filled with rattling bones, has a new celebrity [Bill Clinton consort Gennifer Flowers]. She loves this city, especially the Quarter. Here, a person with scandal in her past does not stand out so much as join in the parade." —*New York Times* reporter Rick Bragg, January, 2002

"The spirit of New Orleans is a spirit of pleasure… The people of New Orleans believe devoutly in their right to drink, dance, gamble, make love, and worship God." —journalist Ernie Pyle, March 7, 1936

Nine Reasons New Orleans is Not in America from travel writer Gene Bourg
1. Before a New Orleanian learns how to cook, he learns how to eat.
2. The municipal motto is "Even if it is broken, don't fix it."
3. Locals wear T-shirts proclaiming "It's Not the Heat, It's the Stupidity."
4. Drivers fight over illegal parking spaces.
5. Speaking in complete sentences is looked on as putting on airs.
6. The law prohibits merchants from holding too many going-out-of-business sales.
7. Drinking on the street is accepted as a fundamental human right.
8. Who else has a singing district attorney (Harry Connick, Sr.)?
9. Where else can you stand on a corner and watch a policeman run a red light on a horse?

New Orleans Beginnings—Actresses Dorothy Lamour and Kitty Carlisle, actors Ed Nelson, Ray Walston, and John Larroquette, musicians Fats Domino, Mahalia Jackson, Wynton Marsalis, Al Hirt, Pete Fountain, and Louis Armstrong, comedian Garrett Morris, author Truman Capote, and journalist Bryant Gumbel

Shreveport

Gangster Ambush—On May 23, 1934, a posse of Texas Rangers ambushed and killed gangsters Bonnie Parker and Clyde Barrow on a quiet country road outside of Shreveport.

Maine

Quips & Quirks

"People in Maine have their own ways of doing things. And if those ways are not always the most efficient, there is usually a reason for them. While the reason may in many cases seem to rest only upon superstition or even narrow-mindedness, it has generally a deeper and firmer foundation. Any bit of folk-wisdom—a cure, a weather or planting sign—does not spring into being spontaneously. It is knowledge gained from experience, tried and found true by generation; therefore it is to be trusted." —*Maine: A Guide Down East,* Federal Writers' Project, 1937

"As goes Maine, so goes the nation." —saying from the 1840 election based on Maine's reflection of the nation's opinions (since becoming a state in 1820, it had voted for the presidential winner in every election except Andrew Jackson's in 1828; for the rest of the 19th century, it only went with the loser four times).

"This is my country, bitter as the sea,
Pungent with the fir and bayberry."
—Maine poet Robert P. Tristram Coffin

Good State for Trivia—Maine is the only state with a one-syllable name and the only one that borders on just one other state.

Largest in New England—At 33,000 sq. miles, Maine is larger than New Hampshire, Vermont, Connecticut, and Rhode Island combined.

Bangor

"There stands the city of Bangor, fifty miles up the Penobscot, at the head of navigation for vessels of the larger class, the principal lumber depot on this continent, with a population of twelve thousand, like a star on the edge of the night, still hewing at the forest of which it is built, already overflowing with the luxuries and refinements of Europe, and sending its vessels to Spain, to England, and to the West Indies for its groceries—and yet only a few axe-men have gone 'up-river' into the howling wilderness which feeds it." —Henry David Thoreau, 1846

Houlton

"I'd like to see how long an Aroostook County [the northernmost county of the mainland] man can stand Florida...in the humid ever-summer I dare his picturing mind not to go back to the shout of color, to the clean rasp of frosty air, to the smell of pine wood burning and the caressing warmth of kitchens. For how can one know color in perpetual green, and what good is warmth without cold to give it sweetness?" —from John Steinbeck's *Travels with Charley*

Portland

"The Atlantic Coast from New York to Portland is an abomination and a curse. It is neither beautiful nor placid, nor is there any enchantment in it. It is one long, hideous summer resort for four hundred miles, with millions of unhappy-looking people running in and out of hot-dog stands in their bathrobes." —journalist Ernie Pyle, August 27, 1935

"At its feet lies Casco Bay with its 365 islands—one for every day in the year—a miniature New England Aegean." —*Maine: A Guide Down East,* Federal Writers' Project, 1937

Stonington

"One doesn't have to be sensitive to feel the strangeness of Deer Isle. And if people who have been going there for many years cannot describe it, what can I do after two days? It is an island that nestles like a suckling against the breast of Maine, but there are many of those. The sheltered darkling water seems to suck up light, but I've seen that before... Stonington, Deer Isle's chief town, does not look like an American town at all in place or in architecture. The resemblance [to the coastal people in West Country England] is doubly strong. [They] are secret people, and perhaps magic people. There's aught behind their eyes, hidden away so deep that perhaps even they do not know they have it. And that same thing is so in Deer Islers. To put it plainly, this Isle is like Avalon; it must disappear when you are not there." —from John Steinbeck's *Travels with Charley*

Maryland

Quips & Quirks

Annapolis

"'George Washington slept here' is no idle boast in Annapolis. He also dined, drank and danced here and frequented the horse races just outside the city gate." —Joyce Gregory Wyels in the March 1999 *Historic Traveler*

But He Wasn't Thrilled About It—Author Alex (*Roots*) Haley's famous ancestor, Kunta Kinte, arrived in Annapolis in 1767.

Baltimore

"Baltimore is the northernmost city in the south, and Washington, D.C., is the southernmost city of the north." —source unknown (see also, Charleston, W.V.)

"I like Baltimore—despite its slicked-up touristy waterfront it remains a seedy old port city, reformable only to a negligible degree." —author Larry McMurtry, *Roads: Driving America's Great Highways*

"The visit was, in some ways, Baltimore's groundhog; a dead-of-winter ritual that held a promise of spring." —from Laura Lippman's novel *In a Strange City*, a mystery revolving around the unknown stranger who appears at Edgar Allan Poe's grave around 3 a.m. every January 19th—Poe's birthday—to leave half a bottle of cognac and three roses

"Baltimore's biggest chain of bookstores is closing. Its flagship public radio station is up for sale. Of the city's two most popular art museums, one hasn't displayed its showpiece collection for nearly two years. The other will soon close most of its galleries until October. And here's how the locals promote the likes of Mozart, Verdi and Puccini: 'Opera. It's better than you think.' If all that doesn't convince you Baltimore is undergoing some sort of prolonged municipal lobotomy, descending into the philistine wallow its detractors have always accused it of inhabiting, then check out the brainless Babbitry appearing these days on public benches: 'Baltimore. The Greatest City in America.' Welcome to the new Indiana, dumber by the minute and proud of it, because our football team can beat yours." —*Baltimore Sun* reporter Dan Fesperman, March 31, 2001

"It's frustrating for me when I hear people say it should be the Colts or nothing. I was heartbroken when the Colts left. But that is in the past. We should move on, and that is the basis of *The Raven*—a man who is mourning his lost love." —Jeff Jerome, curator of the Poe House and Museum at 203 N. Amity St., quoted in the March 28, 1996, *Baltimore Sun.*

Telegraph Destination—On May 24, 1844, Samuel F.B. Morse demonstrated his six-year-old electric telegraph device by sending the message "What hath God wrought?" from Washington, D.C., to Baltimore.

Star Spangled Banner—On a September day during the war of 1812, two men were rowed to a ship anchored in Chesapeake Bay to negotiate the release of an American doctor named William Beanes imprisoned on a British Navy ship. When a battle began early of September 13th, they was detained on the ship, giving one of them, a lawyer, an astonishing view as the British began to shell Fort McHenry, overlooking the harbor. He could tell the British had failed in their efforts to take the fort, because every time the Congreve rockets streaked over the water, he could still see the flag flying over the fort. The lawyer was Francis Scott Key, and the shelling that went from the morning of September 13, 1812, to dawn of the following day was the inspiration for the *Star Spangled Banner.* (Key was an ancestor to author F(rancis) Scott Fitzgerald, who lived in a townhouse on Baltimore's Bolton Hill at 1307 Park Avenue between 1932 and 1935.)

Center of the U.S.—In the 1790 census, the center of the U.S. population was just outside Baltimore.

Beginnings—George Herman "Babe" Ruth was born at 216 Emory St. in Baltimore on February 6, 1895.

Massachusetts

Quips & Quirks

From the Internet: You Live in Massachusetts When...
- The person in front of you is driving 70 mph and you curse him for going too slow.
- You feel that the rest of the world needs to drive more like you.
- The fact that Route 128 and I-95 are pretty much the same thing doesn't confuse you.
- You actually enjoy driving around rotaries.
- You can actually find your way around Boston.
- You almost feel disappointed when someone doesn't flip you the bird when you cut them off or steal their parking space.
- You use colleges as landmarks for directions; e.g., "go past MIT until you hit Harvard. Take a right and go past Lesley. Keep going until you get to Tufts."
- You know that Big Dig is also a kind of ice cream at Brigham's.
- You actually know how to merge from six lanes of traffic down to one.
- You know at least one bar where you can get something to drink after last call.
- When ordering a tonic, you mean a Coke, not quinine water.
- You have never been to Cheers.
- You are proud to drink Sam Adams and think that the rest of the country owes Bostonians a big thank you.
- You knew that there was no chance in hell that the Patriots would move to Hartford.
- You know the Beanpot is a hockey tournament, not a serving dish.
- You know that there are two Bulger brothers.
- You refer to the New York Yankees as the devil's spawn, or worse, and you think Roger Clemens, Wade Boggs, and Derek Jeter are more evil than Whitey Bulger.
- St. Patrick's Day is your favorite holiday; you recognize Evacuation Day as a holiday; and you think the rest of the country owes you for Thanksgiving and Independence Day.
- You know how to pronounce Worcester, Billerica, Haverhill, Barre, and Cotuit.
- You laugh at all the other states in New England.
- You can recognize a girl from Revere simply by her hair.
- You know that there is a bigger difference between Roxbury and West Roxbury than just a compass direction.

- You take it as a compliment when somebody refers to UMass as "ZooMass."
- You put the words "wicked" and "good" together.
- You never go to Cape Cod, but you do go "down the cape."
- You went to Old Sturbridge Village, Plimouth Plantation, or both, on grammar school field trips.
- You're aware that Brimfield has the largest outdoor antique market in the world.
- You can drive to the mountains and the ocean in one day.
- You have a special place in your heart for the Worcester firefighters.
- You know that Mass Pike is some sort of strange dividing line for weather.
- You know that P Town isn't the name of a rap group.
- You know that Ludlow is 90 percent Portuguese and that Fall River is 90 percent Lebanese.
- You do not recognize the letter "R" as part of the English language.

"Massachusetts is parochial, yet it is never long out of the main currents of American life. It is a State of tradition, but part of its tradition is its history of revolt. Its people are fiercely individualistic, yet they have fierce group loyalties. It is noted for conservatism, yet it exports not only shoes and textiles but rebels to all corners of the earth. Its sons and daughters live in small houses, worship in small churches, work in small factories, produce small things, and vote in small political units, yet time and again their largeness of spirit has burst beyond State borders." — *Massachusetts: A Guide to Its Places and People,* Federal Writers' Project, 1937

Amherst
"Fall is here in Amherst, meaning instead of being uncomfortably hot, it's slowly getting uncomfortably cold. But the foliage is beautiful, the Massachusetts air crisp and clear, and the maple syrup still inexpensive." — Adam Lavine, software company executive

The Story of Ramona—Ironically, author Helen Hunt Jackson wrote the moving story of Ramona, an Indian girl living in a California mission, while living at 83 Pleasant St.

Boston
"Whether it be a cleverly executed U-turn into a lonely parking space or just a routine left turn from the right lane of a busy street, the craft and

artistry of a Boston Driver is a sight to behold, preferably at a safe distance."
—from *Wild in the Streets: The Boston Driver's Handbook*

"Boston is a pretty town in a picturesque site on several hills in the middle of the waters." —Alexis de Tocqueville, September 20, 1831

"In Boston, they ask, 'how much does he know?' In New York, 'how much is he worth?' In Philadelphia, 'who were his parents?'" —Mark Twain, 1899

"The Bostonians, almost without an exception, are derived from one country and a single stock. They are all descendants of Englishmen and, of course, are united by all the great bonds of society—language, religion, government, manners, and interest." —Yale President Timothy Dwight, 1796

"As for the legend of ethnic homogeneity, that is so much pernicious twaddle." —a response to Dwight's comment, from *Massachusetts: A Guide to Its Places and People,* Federal Writers' Project, 1937

"We are virtually alone among the states in that our capital city is also our most significant city in terms of culture, sports, population, sin, food, and fun." —unknown Harvard professor

"Nowhere is the poetry of the American past as palpable as it is in the streets of old Boston." —philosopher Simone de Beauvoir, April 18, 1947

"Atlanta is just the opposite of Boston. Boston is a lousy place to live and a great place to visit, while Atlanta is a great place to live and a lousy place to visit." —public relations executive John Day, formerly of Boston and currently of Atlanta

"The city is a beautiful one, and cannot fail, I should imagine, to impress all strangers very favourably." —author Charles Dickens during his 1842 visit

"Here in Boston we build computers that matter. Out in Silicon Valley, they're just building video games." —unnamed Digital Equipment Corp. executive, 1986

"What makes Boston different from other large cities is its sense of community—its walkability, its livability, its sophistication, its sense of scale.

We've got diversity in culture, education, and geography, all on a scale that's appropriate. We feel part of an extended village, not a sprawling city." — Bank of Boston executive vice-president Ira Jackson, quoted in "Best Cities: Where the Living Is Easy," November 11, 1996, *Fortune*

"Boston is famous for being the easiest city in America to get lost in. The streets are so twisty and cut up that you can make one turn, suddenly find the afternoon sun in the east, and swear that somebody must have pushed you." —journalist Ernie Pyle, September 16, 1938

"As a native of the Boston area, I may wish that the Route 128 region turns itself around quickly; as a scholar, I know that it is likely to take decades to overcome the management practices, culture, and institutions that have hindered the region in the past." —AnnaLee Saxenian, in the preface to her study "Regional Advantage"

"In the '80s, Silicon Valley vaulted past the Boston area to become the center of technology and hasn't looked back. Route 128 minicomputer companies like Digital Equipment, Data General, and Wang Computing crumbled amid the tectonics of the computer industry. Boston became an urbane outpost of ingenuity, a place where companies like Cisco Systems set up regional hugs." —from a January 20, 2002, *San Jose Mercury News* editorial entitled, "Sorry, Boston," proclaiming that Boston wasn't going to be the biotech capital either

"Eastern light is never as strong or as full as western light; a thousand McDonalds will not make Boston feel like Tucson." —author Larry McMurtry, *Roads: Driving America's Great Highways*

"The geographical center of Boston is in Roxbury. Due north of the center we find the South End. This is not to be confused with South Boston which lies directly east from the South End. North of the South End is East Boston and southwest of East Boston is the North End." —unknown

Banned in Boston—In the 1920s, the New England Watch and Ward Society (founded in 1918 as a citizens' vigilance group to investigate crime and moral corruption) campaigned against what it considered to be "lewd and indecent" entertainment, whether printed or produced; hence the phrase "Banned in Boston." One such play was Eugene O'Neill's *Strange Interlude*, which instead opened in the town of Quincy (see the entry for Quincy for how this affected a famous hotel chain).

First World Series Game—In October, 1903, the first World Series game was played at the Huntington Avenue Ball Field in Boston. Cy Young's Boston beat Honus Wagner's Pittsburgh five games to three (coincidentally, Cy Young and Honus Wagner both died on December 6, 1955).

Uncivil Disobedience—The evening of December 16, 1773, marked the beginning of increased violence by patriots against England when a group of 150 men dressed as Mohawk Indians threw 342 chests of East India Company tea into Boston harbor, an event that came to be known as the Boston Tea Party.

The Telephone—When Alexander Graham Bell said to Mr. Watson, "Come here. I want you" on March 10, 1876—initiating the first telephone conversation—they were in a laboratory in downtown Boston.

Brookline

Beginnings—35th president John Kennedy was born at 83 Beals St. on May 29, 1917, the first president born in the 20th century.

Cambridge

The First College In America—Harvard was the first college in America, founded in Cambridge in 1636 (followed by College of William and Mary in 1693, Yale in 1701, and the College of New Jersey (Princeton University) in 1746). Five presidents attended Harvard as undergraduates (more than any other university), and four of them were related to each other. Besides John Kennedy, presidential attendees included John Adams and his son John Quincy Adams and Theodore Roosevelt and his cousin Franklin Roosevelt.

Cape Cod

"A man may stand there and put all America behind him." —Henry David Thoreau in *Cape Cod*

Where the Names Came From—Explorer Bartholomew Gosnold named Cape Cod for the fish his crew caught, and named Martha's Vineyard because of the grapes that grew on the island (Martha was his daughter).

Concord

"There's an old cemetery and, less than a mile apart, the hundred-year-old dwellings of the gentle writers of the last century. Besides Thoreau's house, there is the house where Emerson lived lovingly with his second wife and wrote most of his books; here also is one of Nathaniel Hawthorne's houses, and one where Louisa May Alcott spent part of her childhood, dreaming of escape, crushed by the persuasive tyranny of her father, the clergyman, and bearing witness in her timid work to the limitations within which an American woman still managed to something in those days." — philosopher Simone de Beauvoir, April 15, 1947

Beginnings—In 1853, a farmer named Ephraim Bull bred a new strain of grape, named after the community, which inaugurated the commercial production of table grapes in America.

Endings—In Concord's Sleepy Hollow Cemetery, in a swath known as Author's Ridge, Henry Thoreau, Ralph Waldo Emerson, Nathaniel Hawthorne and Louisa May Alcott are all buried.

Deerfield

"To all intents, nothing has happened there for two hundred years; and the whole history of its greatness is crowded into the first three decades of its existence, the violent and dreadful years from 1672 to 1704, when it was the northwest frontier of New England." —*Massachusetts: A Guide to its Places and People,* Federal Writers' Project, 1937

Fall River

One of New England's most infamous murders took place at 92 Second St. on August 4, 1892, in Fall River, inspiring the ditty,

Lizzie Borden took an axe
And gave her mother 40 whacks.
And when she saw what she had done,
She gave her father 41.

Marblehead

"Certain old villages, such as Marblehead, seem untouched since the eighteenth century; they have simply declined. Marblehead was a little town of prosperous ship owners with important dockyards, where the ships were built. The shipyards are dead, and prosperity has vanished, but all the old houses are standing with their little windows rimmed with red or violet." — philosopher Simone de Beauvoir, April 25, 1947

Provincetown

"The spot where the *Mayflower* people first stepped on American soil is right here in Provincetown, and you ought to freeze on to that fact in your guide book, for it's been rising three hundred years now, and most off-Cape folks don't seem to know it yet!" —a Provincetown citizen, quoted in *Massachusetts: A Guide to its Places and People,* Federal Writers' Project, 1937; the ship dropped anchor there on November 11, 1620, after it had been blown off course and abandoned its original destination of Virginia

Quincy

Strange Intervention—When Eugene O'Neill's *Strange Interlude* debuted in Quincy in 1932, across the street from the theater was a restaurant about to go bankrupt. But theatergoers started to patronize the restaurant at intermission, and the proprietor went on to open not only more restaurants but a hotel chain as well. His name was Howard Johnson.

Salem

"In many of these peaceful little villages, in the [late 17th century], they put up wooden stakes for burning witches. I can easily imagine that in these pious colonies of sober houses and honest comfort they felt the need, from time to time, for violent distraction. A society that was obsessed with order and authority and that had enlisted God in its service had to defend itself bitterly against the dangerous mystique of individualism; distrust, foolishness, jealousy, and boredom did the rest." —philosopher Simone de Beauvoir, April 25, 1947

"Come by for a spell." —*the town's tourism slogan*

"Here stored in old landmarks is the romance of swift clipper ships, of bellying sails, of masts stripped for the gale, of sailors' oaths and sailors' roaring chanteys, of ambition and avarice, of mansions built by merchant princes and delicate women nurtured in them." —*Massachusetts: A Guide to its Places and People,* Federal Writers' Project, 1937

Not Customary Activity—It's said that author Nathaniel Hawthorne was inspired to write *The Scarlet Letter* while working at the Salem Customs House, just a few blocks away from the domicile that inspired *The House of the Seven Gables.*

Springfield

Beginnings—James Naismith, a physical education teacher at the YMCA Training School, invented basketball in Springfield in 1891.

Watertown

Horseless Carriage—In September, 1897, brothers Frances and Freelan Stanley drove the first steam-powered vehicle in America down Watertown's Maple Street.

Wellesley

"Near Wellesley I have seen one of the most aristocratic colleges, where they accept students who were rejected elsewhere, and the students lazily pursue their studies in almost luxurious comfort. They live in charming pavilions scattered around the countryside with hardly a care for anything but their appearance and their 'dates.' They have contempt for the Wellesley students, who are equally contemptuous of them." —philosopher Simone de Beauvoir, April 15, 1947

Whitman

A Tasty Story—In 1930, Ruth Graves Wakefield and her husband purchased an inn in Whitman, one that had originally been built in 1709 to house those who collected tolls from travelers between Boston and New Bedford. That gave the Wakefields the inspiration for the name of their property: the Toll House Inn. One day while making a batch of her specialty, Butter Drop Do cookies, Ruth discovered that she was out of bakers chocolate. Remembering that a guest had given her a bar of semi-sweet chocolate, she cut it into pieces and mixed it into the dough, expecting the bits to melt. They didn't, and the cookies with the chocolate bits throughout were a big hit among the inn's guests. The name of the guest who had given Ruth the chocolate bar was Andrew Nestle, and the results were, of course, Toll House cookies.

Worcester

The Teaching President—President John Adams began his professional career as a teacher in Worcester in 1755.

Michigan

Quips & Quirks

"From time to time...the country suddenly changes its look. Just round a wood one sees the elegant spire of a clock tower, houses striking in their whiteness and cleanness, and shops. Two paces further on, the primeval and apparently impenetrable forest reclaims its dominion and again reflects its foliage in the waters of the lake. Those who have passed through the United States will find in this picture a striking emblem of American society. Everything there is abrupt and unexpected; everywhere, extreme civilization borders and in some sense confronts nature left to run riot." —Alexis de Tocqueville, July 19, 1831, on Lake Erie enroute from Buffalo to Detroit

"Northern Michigan is the Maine of the Midwest. The well-to-do of the Midwest, at least the correctly well-to-do, had their summer places there; there is evidence along the lakeshores of the kind of expensive simplicity that prevails in the socially acceptable parts of Maine." —author Larry McMurtry, *Roads: Driving America's Great Highways*

Longest Bridge—Between June 28, 1958, when it surpassed the Golden Gate Bridge, and November 21, 1964, when it was surpassed by the Verrazano Narrows Bridge, the five-mile Mackinac Bridge was the longest suspension bridge in the world.

Where The Names Came From—The four biggest divisions of the largest American car company, General Motors, were either founded by Europeans or named after native Americans: Swiss race-car driver Louis Chevrolet, Scottish plumber David Dunbar Buick, Indian chief Cadillac, and Indian chief Pontiac. Ransom E. Olds was born in Geneva, Ohio, in 1864.

Ann Arbor

"The last bastion of culture in the Midwest." —resident Nancy Volk, formerly of New York, quoted in "The 10 Best Places To Live," July 1996 *Swing*

Largest Stadium—The football stadium at the University of Michigan is the largest at a public school with a capacity of 107,501 (22,001 more than Stanford University Stadium, the largest private school stadium).

Detroit

"Detroit is a dreadful city in a way. It's so big, and it's dirty and smoky with all these auto factories pouring out black clouds, and there are so many poor people here, and the streets are jammed and you have to travel so far to get anywhere. But Detroit has something. It has a personality. You don't sense it at first, but after you're here awhile, you pick it up in people's faces, and the way they talk, and the way they act... Detroit is an emotional city, as an up-again-down-again city would have to be. It goes wild over anything. It worships prize-fighters and symphony orchestras. It does nothing halfway." —journalist Ernie Pyle, November 16, 1935

"It was always a cool city. I've always loved it, mostly because it's an underdog. And I've always rooted for underdogs." —comedian Tim Allen, a native of nearby Birmingham

"Walking through much of downtown Detroit can be like touring a not so amusing ghost town." —*www.lonelyplanet.com*

Pontiac

So Why Can't They Win in the Playoffs?—The Detroit Lions' Silverdome in Pontiac is the largest NFL stadium in the United States, with a capacity of 80,325.

Saginaw

"I find it hard to understand what could induce two foreigners to go to Saginaw. Do you know that Saginaw is the last inhabited point until you come to the Pacific Ocean? I for my sins have been there five or six times, but I had something to gain by doing it and I cannot discover that you have anything to gain." —the unnamed manager of the hotel in Pontiac where Alexis de Tocqueville stayed in July, 1831

"An area of cultivation in the midst of savage tribes and impenetrable forest... The village of Saginaw is the last point inhabited by Europeans to the northwest of the huge peninsula of Michigan. One may regard it as an advanced station, a sort of observation post, which the whites have established in the midst of the Indian tribes." —Alexis de Tocqueville, July, 1831

Minnesota

Quips & Quirks

"We are a state of highly repressed Scandinavians, and sometimes we like to surprise ourselves." —Garrison Keillor, writing in the November 16, 1998, issue of *Time* about the gubernatorial election of former pro wrestler Jesse Ventura

"Minnesotans…evidently thrive on cold, like those ice fisherman who were out with the dawn. I would be the last person on the planet who would voluntarily rise before dawn to go stand on a frozen lake and fish through a hole in the ice, but I can admire the hardiness of people who do." —author Larry McMurtry, *Roads: Driving America's Great Highways*

Split Decision—Minnesota is the only state to have come into the Union in two pieces; the land east of the Mississippi River became part of the U.S. after the Revolutionary War, while the rest followed after the Louisiana Purchase.

Water, Water Everywhere—The largest freshwater lake in the world, Lake Superior is large enough to hold all the other Great Lakes, plus three additional lakes the size of Lake Erie. It's also the home to more than 350 shipwrecks, including the ship memorialized by Gordon Lightfoot, the *Edmund Fitzgerald.*

Advice for Newcomers to Minnesota—The following was purported to have been written by a welcoming committee of Northwest Airlines employees to a group of colleagues being transferred after the closure of a maintenance base in Atlanta.
- At first, you may think snow is pretty. Snow is not pretty. By December you will feel as if you are living in a black-and-white movie. And there is a lot of snow, deep snow that doesn't go away. The reason Northwest Airlines paints its tails red is so they can find the damned things.
- There is no Minnesota cuisine. If it's dead, eat it.
- When you pack to come to Minnesota, you need only to bring one short-sleeved shirt (and that's only in case you want to fly back home for vacation). The short-sleeved shirt season here begins July 26 and is pretty much wrapped up by 3:30 on the 28th.

- Moving on to religion, there are but two faiths here (pro-stadium and anti-stadium). An agnostic is a person who doesn't care whether we have a new stadium or not.
- We have an excellent college system. Unfortunately, it's in Wisconsin, Iowa, or the Dakotas.
- Minnesotans may laugh at you for your backward politics in Georgia. You can stop that with two words: pro wrestler.

Duluth

"Duluth is like a Lilliputian village in a mammoth rock garden. From the western tip of Lake Superior the city rises on rock bluffs 600 to 800 feet above the lake level, houses and business buildings alike dwarfed by the rugged volcanic juttings and the vast expanse of cold blue water." —from *Minnesota, A State Guide*, published by the Works Progress Administration, 1938

Grand Rapids

"She never talked about Minnesota at all. I always thought she was from Hollywood." —actor Mickey Rooney on his teen-age co-star Judy Garland (born in Grand Rapids on June 10, 1922, at what is now 2727 U.S. Hwy. 169 South)

Hibbing

The Hound That Went to Alice—In 1914, a Swedish immigrant named Carl Eric Wickman began transporting miners from Hibbing to Alice for 15 cents each; thus began the Greyhound bus company.

Besides Greyhound—Others natives of Hibbing include attorney Vincent Bugliosi (prosecutor of Charles Manson) and athletes Roger Maris and Kevin McHale; the family of musician Robert Allan Zimmerman moved to Hibbing when he was seven and lived at 2425 7th Ave. East (the 1959 yearbook, from his senior year, is kept under lock and key at the public library, because in 1962, Zimmerman changed his name to Bob Dylan).

Minneapolis

"This house turned out to be Minnesota's version of Graceland. Who knew?" —art historian Evan Maurer, who in 1988 bought the home at 2104 Kenwood Parkway featured in the opening shots of *The Mary Tyler Moore Show*, unaware of how popular the show had been until tourists started showing up the day his family moved in

"With all of its sophisticated trappings—impressive arts institutions, a theater district soaked in bright lights, high-end corporate headquarters—you'd expect to find a district better-than-thou attitude in the City of Lakes. Au contraire. It could be the up-close-and-personal nature scene…the group survival syndrome…or maybe the inherited hospitality from decades of German and Scandinavian immigrants. Those are mere speculative answers to the oft-asked question, 'How come everyone's so NICE?'" —October 1996 *Destinations*

"How good Minneapolis looks may depend on how far out on the prairies you're coming from." —author Larry McMurtry, *Roads: Driving America's Great Highways*

"The Twin Cities are pure heartland USA—industrious and prosperous, heavily into sports, shopping and the great outdoors. Yet they are not carbon-copy twins. St Paul, the state capital, is smaller and quieter, a sedate midsize city spread across gentle rolling hills. Minneapolis, on the other hand, has the nightlife, bars and buzz of an urban oasis." —*www.lonelyplanet.com*

"Even the casual visitor (when he overcomes his bewilderment and determines into which city he has wandered), cannot fail to note certain obvious differences. The St. Paul skyline is all of a piece, Minneapolis sprawls; St. Paul is hilly, Minneapolis level; St. Paul's bridges leap down from the high shore to the loop; in Minneapolis they snake across the river with no regard for distance; St. Paul's loop streets are narrow and concentrated, while in its twin city the center of activity extends many blocks along the along the broad shopping avenues. Minneapolis marks its streets and ornaments its lakes, but leaves its river shore ragged and unkempt below the cream-colored elevators. St. Paul makes much of its river shore but illumines no street sign for a nervous driver. St. Paul has already attained a degree of mellowness and seems to be clinging to its Victorian dignity, while in Minneapolis dignity is less prized than modern spruceness. The visitor from the East will perhaps feel more at home in St. Paul; if from the West he is likely to prefer Minneapolis." —*Minnesota, A State Guide,* published by the Works Progress Administration, 1938

Last Day Game—The last World Series game played during the traditional workday took place at the Minneapolis Metrodome between the Minnesota Twins and the St. Louis Cardinals in 1987; since then, to take advantage of higher ratings, World Series games have been played in prime time or on weekends.

Never Been There Myself—Although the Falls of Minnehaha, part of the Minneapolis' Minnehaha Park, are vividly described in Longfellow's poem *Song of Hiawatha*, Longfellow never saw them in person. He based his description on a daguerreotype done by a Chicago artist that found its way to Cambridge, where the poet lived.

Northwest Angle

"I have never been anyplace where the inhabitants know so little about their own history as the people of Northwest Angle. Not a person I talked with knew why the United States-Canadian boundary was drawn so ludicrously around this isolated spot. The accepted story is that the British surveyors got the Americans drunk, and they drew a line; and then the Americans got the British drunk, and they drew a line... Northwest Angle isn't any bargain, especially. The islands within the American boundary are nice, but they're the poorest in the lake. There are fourteen thousand lakes in Lake of the Woods, which means that thirteen thousand nine hundred of them are in Canada, toward the north and east sides of the lake... The United States got the poorest end of the Lake of the Woods." —journalist Ernie Pyle, August 19, 1936

Rochester

"Had a certain young Englishman [William Worrall Mayo] been content to remain in the chemist's shop where he was employed, Rochester would have undoubtedly developed into a pleasant little trade and railroad center for the farmers whose rich claims surrounded it, and been no better known to the world at large than countless other thriving Middle Western towns. But the year the town was born the English chemist became an American doctor and began a career destined to make this crossroads settlement the world's most renowned privately owned medical center." — from *Minnesota, A State Guide,* published by the Works Progress Administration, 1938

St. Paul

"You have to understand that St. Paul is a pretty laid-back town—they accept bad luck as their due. Like last winter—they were going to have Japanese snow sculptors come in. No one was surprised when there wasn't any snow." —*Minneapolis Star-Tribune* columnist Doug Grow

"Visitors to the Saintly City today seek out the historic homes of novelist F. Scott Fitzgerald and railroad magnate James J. Hill. But to the FBI, St. Paul is better remembered as home to Machine Gun Kelly and dozens of other desperadoes. St. Paul 'was a haven for criminals,' confided a 1934 FBI memo. 'The citizenry knew it, the hoodlum knew it, and every police officer knew it.'" —Crime historian Paul Maccabee in the July 1996 *Historic Traveler*

"If Minneapolis is indeed, as a recent writer puts it, 'a man in the late thirties not quite sure of himself,' then St. Paul is a gracious hostess of 45, who, secure in her mature attractiveness, observes the upward struggles of her neighbors with detached indulgence." —from *Minnesota, A State Guide,* published by the Works Progress Administration, 1938

Winona

Good Thing They Weren't in Bemidji—Actress Winona Ryder was born in Winona on October 29, 1971, and named after the town.

Mississippi

Quips & Quirks

Oxford

Not Quite Telecommuting—When he was under contract to a Hollywood studio, author William Faulkner was working on a screenplay. He found the studio distracting, so he went to the office of the movie's producer and said he would be more productive if he could work at home. The producer, though reluctant to have a writer beyond his beck and call, agreed. His concerns were warranted when during the following days, Faulkner was nowhere to be found in Hollywood. Finally, he called the producer, who demanded to know where he was. "Oxford, Mississippi," answered the author casually. "You said I could work at home, and that's where I am."

Vaughn

Whose Fault Was It?—On the evening of April 30, 1900, a train engineer named John Luther Jones drove his locomotive around a curve near Vaughn and discovered that the last cars of a freight train on a sidetrack hadn't yet cleared the main track. He told his fireman to jump, but kept one hand on the brake and another on the air horn to warn the conductor on the freight train's caboose. The engineer, better known as Casey, was later immortalized in song and fable for his bravery; however, a contemporaneous accident report blames Jones because he was going too fast to give the freight train time to pull onto the main track after his train had passed.

Missouri

Quips & Quirks

Elm Grove

Beginnings—The preferred starting point for westward travel along the Oregon Trail was in Elm Grove, 12 miles southwest of Independence.

Fulton

Where the Term 'Iron Curtain' was Coined—Speaking in the Westminster College gymnasium in Fulton on March 5, 1946, former British Prime Minister Winston Churchill first used the term "Iron Curtain" descending "from Stettin in the Baltic to Trieste in the Adriatic" to describe the isolation of eastern Europe.

Hannibal

"Hannibal has had a hard time of it ever since I can recollect, and I was 'raised' there. First, it had me for a citizen, but I was too young then to really hurt the place." —Mark Twain, in a letter to the *Alta California,* May 26, 1867

Kansas City

"People have this misconception that there's nothing going on here, and it's prairie. It's a great place for artists and musicians. It's an unjaded scene, a little less self-important. I came for the wide open sky and the soothing lifestyle." — Tim Steger, quoted in "The 10 Best Places To Live," July 1996 *Swing*

"I never thought I'd be successful until I was famous in Kansas City." — Walter Cronkite, a native of St. Joseph, Missouri

St. Joseph

Beginnings—When the Pony Express riders took off west, they started from St. Joseph.

It Started With a Poem—In 1871, a 20-year-old newspaperman named Eugene Field took his future wife on a carriage ride along what was then Rochester Road. Years later in London, reportedly homesick for America, he composed a poem called "Lover's Lane, St. Jo." The poem became so famous that Rochester Road was renamed and became the original Lover's Lane.

Endings—Jesse James was gunned down in St. Joseph on April 3, 1882.

St. Louis

"You have punished and ignored virtually every artist who ever came through here." —Kurt Vonnegut

"If you look east through [the Gateway Arch] you just see the squalor of East St. Louis, and if you look west there's the mass of downtown St. Louis. You cannot look through it and see the west, despite which the Gateway Arch remains a great thing. In my mind's eye, when I drive past it, I keep transferring it to a lonely bluff upriver; to allow the eye to be tempted as one negotiates the fast, mean interchanges of downtown St. Louis is to invite instant smashup." —author Larry McMurtry, *Roads: Driving America's Great Highways*

"Sometimes I am reminded of Brigadoon. When I am within the city borders, I cannot quite imagine the rush and whirl of the outside world, and when I am away, the easy friendliness and slow pace of St. Louis seem something of a dream." —travel writer Tim Page in the July 2, 2000 *Washington Post*

"I cannot think of any city more cultured than St. Louis." —poet Marianne Moore, who was born there in 1887

"In the old French portion of the town the thoroughfares are narrow and crooked, and some of the houses are very quaint and picturesque: being built of wood, with tumble-down galleries before the windows, approachable by stairs, or rather ladders, from the street. There are queer little barbers' shops, and drinking-houses too, in this quarter; and abundance of crazy old tenements with blinking casements, such as may be seen in Flanders. Some of these ancient habitations, with high garret gable windows peeking into the roofs, have a kind of French shrug about them; and, being lop-sided with age, appear to hold their heads askew besides, as if they were grimacing in astonishment at the American Improvements." —author Charles Dickens during his 1842 visit

"First in booze, first in shoes, and last in the American League." —a description of St. Louis in the days of the Browns, its hapless baseball team that in 1953 left to become the Baltimore Orioles

"The first time I ever saw St. Louis, I could have bought it for six million dollars, and it was the mistake of my life that I did not do it." —Mark Twain in *Life on the Mississippi*

"If you send a damned fool to St. Louis, and you don't tell them he's a damned fool, they'll never find out." —Mark Twain in *Life on the Mississippi*

"St. Louis and the Mississippi affected me like no other place on earth." —T.S. Eliot (grandson of the founder of Washington University)

"That city of outward-bound caravans for the West, which is to the prairies what Cairo is to the Desert." —from Herman Melville's *Mr. Parkman's Tour*

Most Inaccurate Headline—It was in St. Louis' Union Station that election victor Harry Truman was photographed holding up the November 2, 1948, copy of the Chicago Tribune incorrectly headlined "Dewey Beats Truman."

Montana

Quips & Quirks

"I only have to be in Montana—any part—about ten minutes to reconvince myself that it is easily the most beautiful American state... If one's passion is high plains travel, U.S. 2 is as good as it gets. The hay fields were golden, the plowed land a rich brown, the Missouri bluffs bluish, the sky a deeper blue, the thunderheads a brilliant white, the hummocky, rolling rangeland a somber gray. The colors, all subtle except the thunderheads, were constantly shifting and recombining as the clouds blocked and then released the strong sunlight." —author Larry McMurtry, *Roads: Driving America's Great Highways*

"Like many fly fisherman in western Montana where the summer days are almost Arctic in length, I often do not start fishing until the cool of the evening. Then in the Arctic half-light of the canyon, all existence fades to a being with my soul and memories and the sounds of the Big Blackfoot River and a four-count rhythm and the hope that a fish will rise. Eventually, all things merge into one, and a river runs through it. The river was cut by the world's great flood and runs over rocks from the basement of time. On some of those rocks are timeless raindrops. Under the rocks are the words, and some of the words are theirs. I am haunted by waters." —from the opening narration of *A River Runs Through It*

"On the drive down into Montana from its northern border, it is not immediately clear what has attracted a whole posse of high-profile pioneers—led by Ted Turner and Jane Fonda, David Letterman, and the legendary quarterback John Elway—to set up homes in the state. The landscape is big and tough, but no more remarkable than in other parts of the Wild West. And the businesses which line the roadside on the journey along the Flathead Valley to Whitefish seem oddly ill-fitted to the needs of the new-age rancher. It is easy enough to get a muffler fixed, buy liquor, or eat breakfast at any time of day; but in 50 miles you don't pass a single health-food store, cappuccino bar or Subaru dealership." —travel writer Stephen Wood in the March 17, 2001, *London Independent*

"I am in love with Montana. For other states I have admiration, respect, recognition, even some affection, but with Montana it is love... It seems to me that Montana is a great splash of grandeur. The scale is huge but not overpowering. The land is rich with grass and color, and the mountains are the kind I would create if mountains were ever put on my agenda. Montana seems to me to be what a small boy would think Texas is like from hearing Texans." —John Steinbeck, *Travels with Charley*

"Pretty soon you won't recognize the place. We're selling off Montana piece by piece to out-of-staters. These people are changing it before our very eyes. On many of these ranchettes you can't hunt and fish any more. You can't fish and you can't have access." —Montana congressman Bob Gilbert

"Everywhere you go you see trailer homes, shanties, broken down cars, old people without any money. The lumber industry's dead. With the price of red meat way down, the big cattle ranches are in trouble. The Rocky Mountains can't support their traditional industries any longer. The stereotype of the Montana cowboy is in reality that of a man riding out to the unemployment lines. And so it's not all that surprising that he wants to sell his land—he doesn't have much of a choice, and the land is just about all he's got. So he sells it, in small parcels, which is all that's wanted. And often he sells to city folks who want peace and quiet and beauty and wild animals and fishing and hiking. And look what happens? These people buy the land, and go crazy about it. Round here they pay $3,000 an acre—good money. So the old rancher who thought he was down on his luck walks away with six million bucks in his pocket. Now that's not bad, is it? And so who loses? The rancher's happy. The new guy's happy. The Valley gets richer because of all the money that's being spent. This opposition comes from a bunch of cockamamie idealists, people who are stuck in time with Wells Fargo, or Lewis and Clark, or General Custer and Sitting Bull, and who just don't want things to change. Well, guys, I say—wake up and smell the coffee. America's changing—and so is Montana, even old Montana." —a Hamilton real estate agent, quoted in the February 15, 1992, *London Guardian*

"I wish that every state historical society in America would send a delegation to Montana. They might also invite a few writers of history textbooks along. And if they would then practice what they learned, I'll bet that twenty years from now we Americans would know a lot more about American history... [With its historical markers,] Montana makes history a thing of joy, instead of a stodgy sermon." —journalist Ernie Pyle, October 9, 1936

Fourth Largest—Montana is the fourth largest state, after Alaska, Texas, and California.

First Congresswoman—On November 7, 1916, Montana's Jeannette Rankin became the first woman elected to Congress.

Butte

"Beautiful audience. Compact, intellectual, and dressed in perfect taste. It surprised me to find this London-Parisian-New York audience out in the mines." —Mark Twain, August 1, 1895, after a speaking engagement at the Butte opera house

"A mile high, a mile deep, and where everyone is on the level." —a saying about the city because it sat 5,280 feet above sea level, had underground copper mines that went as deep as a mile below the surface, and had a reputation for people who dealt squarely with friends and strangers alike.

"An island of easy money entirely surrounded by whisky." —Jere Murphy, police chief of Butte in its heyday as a wide open town where drinking, gambling, and prostitution were common

"Butte, Montana, is the place where the Wild West married the Industrial Revolution." —Dan Baum and Meg Knox in the January 1992 *Smithsonian*

Where Keno Began in America—Just as they helped build the Union Pacific railroad, Chinese immigrants also worked in the copper mines of Montana. From China, they brought several games of chance, including a lottery game where players sought to match 10 Chinese characters from a group of 80. Sound like the Keno that's played in Nevada casinos? It should—the manager of a Butte cigar store named Francis Lyden took the game to Reno when gambling was legalized there in 1935. What was known as Keno then is what we think of as bingo today, its name derived from the Latin word for five, *quine* (indicating the five-by-five numbers on a card), plus the suffix -o from *lotto*. The game we know today went through a series of names until it wrested the name Keno. It was Joe Lyden, however, who took the game to Las Vegas in 1956 and created the game we know today; he replaced numbered maple balls with ping-pong balls, inaugurated the electronic board to reveal the numbers, and, perhaps most importantly for its popularity, started holding drawings every 15 minutes instead of once a day.

Great Falls

"Great Falls is one of the prettiest towns in the West, resembling Denver of a few years ago, except that the buildings are finer than those in Denver." —Mark Twain, arriving in Great Falls on July 31, 1895

Missoula

"This is the opposite of New York; an outpost of liberalism in a state that has, perhaps, more than its share of right-wing crazies. It is a great place to live the contemplative life, enriched by hikes, canoe trips, mountain biking, sunsets, and whatever the University of Montana has to offer, which is plenty." —syndicated columnist Donald Kaul

Author John Updike dubbed Missoula the "Paris of the '90s," a flattering but somewhat gross exaggeration. —*www.montana.com/missoula/*

Wheeler

"You have to see the town of Wheeler to believe it. When you drive through, you think somebody must have set up hand-painted store fronts on both sides of the road, as background for a Western movie thriller. But it's real. Wheeler is today the wildest Wild West town in North America. Except for the autos, it is a genuine throwback to the 1880s, to Tombstone and Dodge city and Goldfield." —journalist Ernie Pyle, September 17, 1936

Beginnings—On November 23, 1936, the first cover of Life magazine featured a photograph of the Fort Peck Dam on the Missouri River, not far from Wheeler.

Nebraska

Quips & Quirks

"They think we don't have teeth—that we're not civilized out here. And we are." —sophomore Amanda Becker, University of Nebraska at Kearney, 2000

"God bless Nebraska—I love the state—but it's boring. There's not a lot to do, especially in wintertime." —North Bend native and actress Marg Helgenberger, quoted in the February 2002 *Biography*

"Nebraskans...spend much of their time convincing people that the state has modern amenities (like cars), includes professions other than farming, and can, in fact, be located on a map... Few people realize it, but their lives wouldn't be the same without Nebraska. There'd be no Kool-aid, no Reuben sandwiches. And ATMs? Forget about it. Without us, there'd be no Henry Fonda or Malcolm X. Even Johnny Carson spent his formative years here, which is appropriate, since this is the state that invented the TV dinner." —staff writer Kim Campbell in the December 7, 2000, *Christian Science Monitor*

"You could find the Missouri River easily on the television networks' electoral maps last week: right where the Bush red of Nebraska butted up against the Gore blue of Iowa. To people on the coasts, Iowa and Nebraska may seem identical—long stretches of Interstate 80 with too much corn and not a single mountain. In many ways, though, and especially on Election Day, the Cornhusker and Hawkeye States are as different as, well, the Cornhuskers and the Hawkeyes... 'There's a poured concrete wall, about 8 feet wide, almost impenetrable, that rises up out of the middle of the Missouri River about 40 feet high. It's invisible, but it's very real,' said Dan Offenburger, the former Creighton University athletic director who has returned to his hometown of Shenandoah, Iowa.'" —reporter Stephen Buttry in the November 13, 2000, *Omaha World-Herald*

Omaha
"I do love Omaha. I often wish I were back here. And I always think of myself as the girl who was found at the Community Playhouse...in a trunk maybe." —actress Dorothy McGuire, 1950

"It's virtually a *tabula rasa*. No one knows anything about it." —researcher Stanley C. Plog who tallied 10,000 responses about what

Americans thought of Nebraska; one question asked respondents to rank cities they'd like to visit again, and Omaha came in second to last, just above Detroit

"We knew going into this that we didn't have an image, but we didn't know the depth of the problem." —Tim McNeil, manager of marketing for the Omaha Convention and Visitors Bureau, which commissioned the Plog study

"For a town that produced Henry Fonda, Marlon Brando, and Fred Astaire, I'm a sad commentary, I'll tell you." —investor Warren Buffett, quoted in the June 16, 1998, *Omaha World-Herald*

"Omaha…is a plain little town, so unassuming that it still calls its airport an airfield." —author Larry McMurtry, *Roads: Driving America's Great Highways*

Beginnings—Grand Island native Henry Fonda dropped out of the University of Minnesota after two years and had returned home to Nebraska in 1925. A friend of his mother's nevertheless thought he had talent and convinced him to join her Omaha Community Playhouse (where native Dorothy McGuire also got her start). That friend knew something about talent, presumably. She was Marlon Brando's mother, Dorothy (the actor was born in Omaha on April 3, 1924).

Red Cloud

"As I looked about me, I felt that the grass was the country, as the water is the sea…and there was so much motion in it, the whole country seemed somehow, to be running." —*My Antonia* author Willa Cather, who moved to Red Cloud from Virginia when she was 10

Wahoo

Beginnings—Darryl F. Zanuck, founder of the 20th Century Fox film studio, was born in Wahoo on September 5, 1902.

Nevada

Quips & Quirks

"Nevada was never burdened with the puritanical prohibitions that weigh on the other states: gambling, the sale of liquor, nightlife, and divorce are all authorized here, as is prostitution—at least on the outskirts of town. This licentiousness, a result of the land's poverty, has become the source of its wealth." —philosopher Simone de Beauvoir, March 7, 1947 (actually, gambling was illegal in Nevada for the 20 years prior to 1931; prostitution is still illegal in Washoe and Clark Counties, home to Reno and Las Vegas)

Las Vegas

"Sinatra started Las Vegas. I guess Disney will finish it." —singer Robert Goulet

"Las Vegas blossoms from the blank face of the desert. Pockmarked with vacant hardscrabble expanses, the city seems unfinished—a quivering, pulsating conglomeration of potential." —Howard Baldwin from a 1986 travel article, "Take a Gamble"

"You go to Vegas to escape and become anonymous. It's the perfect place for a crime drama." —Anthony Zuiker, creator of *CSI: Crime Scene Investigation.*

"The clubs are much like those in Reno: the same lit-up signs evoking the gold rush period, the same games, the same lotteries all marinating in the stench of alcohol and tobacco." —philosopher Simone de Beauvoir, March 10, 1947

"Las Vegas demands the suspension of disbelief—the moment you start to take it seriously you miss the point. It's glitz for its own sake, over-the-top hustle and flash as means and end. It's crowds of people in polyester pantsuits, big hair and gold chains, staring at neon signs and spinning lemons like deer hypnotized by headlights." —*www.lonelyplanet.com*

"We were in Vegas, a truly terrible town in which day is night and night is a complete gross-out. [We] completed our work on the sales floor about 7 p.m. and headed out for some drinks, followed by cocktails, succeeded by a nightcap or two. Perhaps there was good in there somewhere, but back then, in the mid-'90s, Vegas wasn't really all that big on food." —*Fortune* columnist Stanley Bing, February 4, 2002

"A boom town of swimming pools and air conditioning amid the desert, Las Vegas owes its very existence to the idea that we can reshape the world to make it more convenient for us." —*San Jose Mercury-News* writer Hal Kahn, reporting on his first visit to Las Vegas, 1996

"Las Vegas is no ghost town just because the dam is finished. It is a little metropolis, and always will be. It's the only town of any size for at least two hundred miles in any direction. Tourists, business travelers, ranchers, miners, and just plain desert rats keep its streets always colorful and fairly crowded." —journalist Ernie Pyle, March 30, 1938

"Like Los Angeles, its bigger and older sister, Las Vegas is for many a hard city to love. It's about as quaint as spandex. Say postwar here and you're probably referring to the Persian Gulf." —*Sunset,* 1998

Q: "If it's noon in New York City, what time is it in Las Vegas?"
A: "1962."
—KNPR disk jockey Brian Sanders

"The Circus-Circus is what the whole hep world would be doing on Saturday night if the Nazis had won the war." —from Hunter S. Thompson's *Fear and Loathing in Las Vegas*

"Las Vegas is the most extreme and allegorical of American settlements, bizarre and beautiful in its venality and in its devotion to immediate gratification, a place the tone of which is set by mobsters and call girls and ladies' room attendants with amyl nitrite poppers in their uniform pockets." —Joan Didion in "Marrying Absurd," from *Slouching Toward Bethlehem*

"Here is Truth, as defined in some of the lustier parts of the Mojave Desert: If big is good, bigger is better, and if gaudy is good, gaudier is even more so. Say howdy to Las Vegas, the City on Steroids. Las Vegas has always been a little eccentric. It is, after all in the middle of nowhere, makes its living from sex and gambling and has the worst drivers anywhere outside San Francisco. But it's beyond eccentric these days. Way beyond. There's only one credo in this town today: Build it taller, wider, bigger, sexier and more expensive. And what isn't being built is being torn down and replaced, or expanded." —*San Jose Mercury-News* travel editor Zeke Wigglesworth, October 1996

Laughlin

"The Wal-Mart of casino towns." —Humorist Joe Bob Briggs

Reno

"Downtown Reno is a sight to behold on Saturday night. It is a genuine cross between Hollywood and Broadway, with a touch of the West thrown in. The streets are jammed. You can hardly bear the leap and flash and glare of the great colored neon signs. There are autos by the hundreds, most of them from California." —journalist Ernie Pyle, November 22, 1937

"America is a box full of surprises, but Reno is one of the greatest astonishments for me. Associating this name with Hollywood, I imagined a luxurious Monte Carlo populated with glittering move stars. And I fall in to a crude western town." —philosopher Simone de Beauvoir, March 7, 1947

Divorce Central—In the early 1900s, hoping to draw business from neighboring California, the Nevada Legislature voted to allow a six-month waiting period for divorce (half what it was in California), launching Reno's reputation as the divorce capital of the world. In 1927, the waiting period was reduced to three months, but after Idaho and Arkansas matched that, in March 1931 the Legislature voted to reduce the waiting period down to a short six weeks.

Virginia City

Beginnings—It was here in 1862 that a reporter from Missouri began writing for the local newspaper. He chose a pen name, something the steamboat captains used to call on the Mississippi when they gauged the depth of the river, and thus Samuel Clemens became Mark Twain.

New Hampshire

Quips & Quirks

"New Hampshire folks are the merriest of the Puritans." —author Cornelius Weygandt, in the opening essay to *New Hampshire: A Guide to the Granite State* (this statement that can only be taken as ironic, because this installment of the Federal Writers' Project series is quite dry; in contrast, *Vermont: A Guide to the Green Mountain State* is quite witty)

"New Hampshire is America's Canada, with most of the population hugging the Massachusetts border...with a simplistic image that belies the complexities, with a great backyard of woods and hills that shapes the views and perspectives of the people who haven't even ventured there, and with a sense of place so firm so robust, so large that it works its will on newcomer and native alike." —journalist David M. Shribman, writing in the January 30, 2000, *Boston Globe*

"They are friendliness itself when you know them. They have a way of sticking to their purposes and to you when you have won their friendship. It is granite that holds longest after nightfall the heat of the sun." —author Cornelius Weygandt, in the opening essay to *New Hampshire: A Guide to the Granite State*

Bretton Woods

Where The World Bank Started—During most of the month of July in 1944, representatives of 44 nations met at the Mt. Washington Hotel in Bretton Woods to plan a postwar economical agreement that spawned the World Bank and the International Monetary Fund.

Conway

"It's the winters. I've never gotten my way around them. Bein' holed up hard for six months can get ya kinda fidgety. Still haven't gotten under the skin of the place. Folks is friendly enough, but they keep themselves to themselves." —a propane salesman identified only as Clyde by Joanna Symons in the May 1, 1999, *London Daily Telegraph*

Cornish

The Most Famous Recluse—J.D. Salinger's home town. He likes his privacy. Don't visit him.

Derry

"To a large extent, the terrain of my poetry is the Derry landscape, the Derry farm. Poems growing out of this, though composite, were built on incidents and are therefore biographical. There was something about the experience at Derry which stayed in my mind and was tapped for poetry in the years that came after." —poet Robert Frost, who spent 11 years there starting in 1900

Exeter

"Ten miles east of Exeter are the waters of the Atlantic Ocean. When the wind is 'in the east,' the tang of the sea is strong. This has given Exeter somewhat of the spirit of Gloucester or Marblehead, which is also evident in the architecture and the arrangement of the streets." —*New Hampshire: A Guide to the Granite State,* Federal Writers' Project, 1937

Keene

"[Keene is] noted for kindly hospitality, culture without pretense, and breeding without conventionality." —historian Francis Parkman

New Jersey

Quips & Quirks

"It's in New Jersey? I hate New Jersey! I'm sorry they ever finished the George Washington Bridge." —Walter Matthau as Willy Clark in *The Sunshine Boys*

"Jersey is short, tough, and looking for a fight. That's because everyone wants our women. Sure, they pretend to want the California girl, all blond and Barbie and demurely flirtatious. But the Jersey girl, with her big hair and stone-washed jeans, takes Barbie's lunch money. If there were a New Jersey Barbie, her clothes would come off even faster than regular Barbie's." —*Time* columnist Joel Stein

So Close—New Jersey is the fourth smallest state, after Vermont, Rhode Island, and Delaware. It was the third state to ratify the constitution, after Delaware and Pennsylvania came first. Newark, founded in 1666, is the third oldest city in America, after New York and Boston.

Atlantic City

"It's a shame you never saw Atlantic City when it had floy-floy... That was something special. Atlantic City had floy-floy coming out of its ears in those days. Now it's all so goddamn legal. Howard Johnson's running a casino." —Burt Lancaster as numbers runner Lou Pasco in *Atlantic City*

And the Dentists Cheered—While no one knows exactly who was the first person to make and sell salt water taffy, or even whether that person was in Atlantic City—since there are records of it being sold both there and in the Midwest in 1880—but it was Joseph Fralinger, an Atlantic City vendor, who first packaged it in boxes and sold it as a traditional beach souvenir.

Elberon

Death of a President—James Garfield died in Elberon on September 19, 1881, after he had been shot at the Washington, D.C., train station the previous July 2nd.

Glassboro

Little Progress—Lyndon Johnson and Alexei Kosygin met here on June 23, 1967, but made little progress on the issues they discussed: Vietnam, the Middle East, and the spread of nuclear weapons.

Hoboken

"Hoboken has a Rip Van Winkle quality to it. It's like it just went to sleep in the 1930s." —resident Diane Garden in the November 15, 1985, *New York Times*

Old Blue Eyes' Hometown—Singer Frank Sinatra was born in Hoboken on December 12, 1915, and grew up at 841 Garden St.

Before Flow-Through Bags—Lipton Tea was imported into the U.S. from England at a wharf in Hoboken; Sir Thomas Lipton was even a member of the Hoboken Chamber of Commerce.

The First Twist-Off Top—In 1912, Nabisco tried to address the increasing demand for English-style cookies with three new brands. The first two—Mother Goose and Veronese—have been lost to history, but the third one was a whopping success: Oreo. Unfortunately, what has been lost to history for the Oreo is just what the heck its name means.

Jersey City

"We're so fragmented now; there are parts of this county where nobody reads us. They talk about New York being diverse, but they haven't been to Hudson County." —Earl Morgan, columnist for the *Jersey Journal,* noting that county schoolchildren speak some 52 languages, in the January 14, 2002, *Washington Post*

Lakehurst

Last Night of the Hindenburg—The zeppelin Hindenburg was landing at the Lakehurst Naval Air Station on the evening of May 6, 1937, when its hydrogen fuel exploded, destroying the ship and the future of the zeppelin as a mode of transportation.

New Brunswick

Beginnings—Actor Michael Douglas was born in New Brunswick on September 25, 1944.

Princeton

"Through the window, we can see the great lawns and rising buildings of the university. Flowers, grass, and terraces dominate a vast area, giving this studious retreat the luxury of a royal resident. The medieval pomp of the dining hall and the sitting rooms is worthy of a refined prince. In the midst

of the dignified furniture, paintings, tapestries, and cupboards, it's odd to see young people in checked shirts, smoking, with their feet on the tables."
—philosopher Simone de Beauvoir, April 24, 1947

Endings—Albert Einstein died in Princeton on April 18, 1955.

The Lindbergh Kidnapping—On the evening of March 2, 1932, Charles Lindbergh's 20-month-old son and namesake was kidnapped from his crib in the family home at Hopewell, not far from Princeton. Almost two years later, immigrant Bruno Hauptmann was found guilty at the Flemington court house and sentenced to die for the crime. His wife maintained his innocence until the day she died at 95 in 1994.

Where The Martians Landed—When Orson Welles panicked America with a radio broadcast of H.G. Wells' *War of the Worlds,* the fictional landing spot of the Martians was outside Princeton.

The First Campus—The first university to refer to its land as a "campus" was Princeton, it was the fourth university founded in America, after Harvard, College of William and Mary, and Yale. Originally the College of New Jersey, its site was chosen because it was halfway between William and Mary and Yale.

Weehawken

Endings—On July 11, 1804, Alexander Hamilton met vice-president Aaron Burr's challenge to duel after Hamilton had insulted Burr at a dinner party and word of it ended up in an Albany, N.Y., newspaper (they had previously feuded over many larger political issues). When they met at the dueling grounds in Weehawken (about 5 miles north of Jersey City), Hamilton's shot missed but Burr's didn't. Hamilton died the following day.

New Mexico

Quips & Quirks

"If you ever go to New Mexico, it will itch you for the rest of your life."
—photographer Georgia O'Keefe

Ajo

"Just before I came to Ajo I noticed an odd geological development, an area of tiny buttes, most of them only twenty or thirty feet high… It's as if Monument Valley had been miniaturized and set down in the Sonoran desert, for those who haven't time to visit the big valley to the north." — author Larry McMurtry, *Roads: Driving America's Great Highways*

Alamagordo

"There is nothing like the White Sands anywhere in the world. They are an albino Sahara. They are miles of drifted sugar. They are an ocean of utter white. They astound you and they give you the creeps." —journalist Ernie Pyle, December 7, 1939

Albuquerque

"Albuquerque, home of the Lovelace Clinic, was a dirty red sod-hut tortilla desert city that was remarkably short on charm, despite the Mexican touch here and there." —Tom Wolfe in *The Right Stuff*

Second to Denver—At 4,955 feet, Albuquerque is the second-highest major city in the U.S.

Roswell

"The 'Roswell Incident' refers to an event that supposedly happened in July, 1947, wherein the Army Air Forces (AAF) allegedly recovered remains of a crashed "flying disc" near Roswell, New Mexico. In February, 1994, the General Accounting Office (GAO), acting on the request of a New Mexico Congressman, initiated an audit to attempt to locate records of such an incident and to determine if records regarding it were properly handled… Research revealed that the 'Roswell Incident' was not even considered a UFO event until the 1978-1980 time frame. Prior to that, the incident was dismissed because the AAF originally identified the debris recovered as being that of a weather balloon. Subsequently, various authors wrote a number of books claiming that, not only was debris from an alien spacecraft recovered, but also the bodies of the craft's alien occupants. These claims continue to evolve today and the Air Force is now routinely accused of engaging in a 'cover-up' of this supposed event." —from the executive summary of the Air Force's 1994 report on Roswell (http://www.af.mil/lib/roswell.html)

"The U.S. government covered it up, [Karl] Pflock believes, not because it was an alien spacecraft but because the balloon experiment was a Cold War secret... A careful comparison of eyewitness accounts with recently declassified documents of a secret research project called Mogul appear to answer the question... The Mogul researchers were seeing whether it would be possible to use balloons to listen for high-altitude echoes of Soviet nuclear tests. "The bulk of what they remember," Pflock said of the eyewitnesses who actually saw the debris, "matches project Mogul... Roswell has just become an absolutely whale-sized red herring." —from "Bringing Roswell Incident Back to Earth," by *Albuquerque Journal* reporter John Fleck, July 31, 2001

Santa Fe

"I don't know of a town in America that has such astoundingly long unfoldings of nature as you see from just outside Santa Fe." —journalist Ernie Pyle, January 12, 1937

"Santa Fe makes me think of Saint-Tropez, with the Indians playing (somewhat more mysteriously) the role of the native fisherman, whose trousers and slicers are imitated by the tourists." —philosopher Simone de Beauvoir, March 20, 1947

"I think New Mexico was the greatest experience from the outside world that I ever had... The moment I saw the brilliant, proud morning shine high over the deserts of Santa Fe, something stood still in my soul." —author D.H. Lawrence, who went on to Taos in the early 1920s at the invitation of patron Mabel Dodge Luhan in the hopes of helping his tuberculosis

Second Oldest—Santa Fe is the second oldest city in the U.S., after St. Augustine, Fla.

Why

"Most people, finding themselves in Why, will be likely to question the fact that they are there. Why is hot, dry, dusty, and without amenities of any sort. Some of the trailer houses scattered around the outskirts have been there so long that they look like volcanic encrustations of some kind." — author Larry McMurtry, *Roads: Driving America's Great Highways*

New York

Quips & Quirks

"A majority of the people from the South voted to sell New York. That figures, but apparently people from the Northeast didn't reciprocate. A majority of the people from the Northeast voted to sell New Jersey, one of their own." —from Andy Rooney's "Special Sale Today: New York," an article reporting on the results from a poll he commissioned to find out which state people would want to sell to pay off the national debt.

Big Stretch—New York is the only state that touches both the Atlantic Ocean and the Great Lakes.

Albany
"Of all the miserable, wretched, second-class, one-horse towns, this is the most miserable." —architect H.H. Richardson, originator of the Richardson Romanesque style, 1870

"Albany, the Beverwyck, the Willemstadt, the Fort Orange of Colonial times—the oldest city in the United States except St. Augustine—has a claim to the reverence not only of every true-hearted Dutchman who loves his pipe, his kraut, and his freedom, but of the universal Yankee nation, which has no geographical limit this side of Saturn's rings." —*Harper's New Monthly Magazine*, 1857

"The Americans have such a fear of centralization and of the power of capitals, that they almost always take care to put the seat of legislative and executive power far from the capitals. Thus the seat of the legislature and government of the State of New York is at Albany; the seat of the government of Pennsylvania is at [Harrisburg], a little town in the interior of the country, and not at Philadelphia; that of Maryland at Annapolis and not at Baltimore." —Alexis de Tocqueville, October 25, 1831 (the two exceptions to this rule are Boston and Denver)

"To me the city remains a slice of frozen time. The imprint of a grand heyday lurks staunchly, eloquently, in the trills of a wrought-iron handrail on a historic brownstone, the early September light on the ornate State Capitol, and the still-legible sign painted on the rough brick of a downtown building, proclaiming in vain that the best-dressed man still wore a particular brand of suit." —journalist Jill Schensul, writing in the *Hackensack, N.J. Record*

Bethel

Musical History—Even though it's gone down in history as Woodstock, the August 1969 music festival took place at Max Yasgur's farm in Bethel.

Binghamton

"Rod Serling and Binghamton were perfect for each other. Each projected a persona that gave little hint of the ironies hidden beneath. A sublayer of subtle but insidious anti-Semitism affected all Jews in Binghamton's small-city 'perfect harmony,' including the Serlings. Likewise, Serling's carefree, buyout, easy-going exterior hid a very real sense of desperation." —Joel Engel, in Serling's biography *Rod Serling: The Dreams and Nightmares of Life in the Twilight Zone*

Bronx

And He Didn't Even Use His Hands—Originally, the New York Yankees shared the Polo Grounds (yes, they were originally used for polo) with the New York Giants baseball team, whose owners controlled the stadium. But when Babe Ruth joined the Yankees, his home-run prowess began drawing bigger crowds for Yankee games than for Giants games, so the Giants' owners kicked out the team. Its owners built Yankee Stadium, almost directly across the Harlem River from the Polo Grounds at 155th Street, and it thereby became known as "The House That Ruth Built." (The Giants deserted the Polo Grounds in 1958 for San Francisco, and the Mets played there for two seasons until Shea Stadium was completed, also in the Bronx.)

Buffalo

"Jim Kelly's contract with the Bills is for $7.5 million. That's $500,000 to play football and $7 million to live in Buffalo." —Ralph Hasty, San Jose DJ

"He might not enjoy Buffalo, but he'll enjoy playing for Buffalo." —New England Patriots linebacker Mike Vrabel on Drew Bredsoe's move from the Patriots to the Bills

"No city, save one, owes so much to railroads as does Buffalo. Her terminal facilities are unequaled, and her transfer yards at East Buffalo are the largest in the world, with the outlying country encompassed for miles about by a net-work of tracks, approaching closer and closer as they near the city, and extending around the harbor-side to pour their freight of coal, salt, and petroleum in to the lake vessels in return for a cargo of grain, flour, lumber, iron, and copper ore. Commercial Buffalo is like a portly and self-satisfied spider, supreme in the centre of her web." —*Harper's New Monthly Magazine,* 1885

"After a quick lunch, I gather up my courage and go out for a walk. I would like to see the lake. I walk down Main Street, against the wind. The sidewalk becomes confusing terrain, the half-frozen mud slippery beneath my feet. Depots, warehouses, rails, abandoned hulls of great ships—I am walking in a no-man's-land that is neither port nor station, nor town. Far away you can see the lake, but there's no way of getting to it." —philosopher Simone de Beauvoir, February 19, 1947

"A woman [called me] who wanted to fly to Hippopotamus, N.Y. After assuring her there was no such place, she became irate and said it was a big city with a big airport. I asked if Hippopotamus was near Albany or Syracuse. It wasn't. Then I asked if it was near Buffalo. 'Buffalo!' she said. 'I knew it was a big animal.'" —airline reservations agent Jonathan Lee in the September 16, 1985, *Travel Weekly*

"This upstate port on the shores of Lake Erie offers much more than wings, waterfalls, snowstorms and Bills. Architecturally speaking, Buffalo is one of the most diverse and sophisticated cities in the country." —Steve Jordan in the July/August 2000 *Old House Journal.*

"I'll take its wings over Chi-town's hot dogs, Bills fans over Bears fans, the Darwin D. Martin House Complex over the Wright houses in Oak Park, kazoos over the South Side blues. Well, that might be overstating it. But I can stomach a pretty long kazoo solo if it's played on the way to Niagara Falls." —Chris King in the September 2001 *Car & Travel Monthly*

The Biggest for Three Years—With a capacity of 80,025, the Buffalo Bills' Rich Stadium (now Ralph Wilson Stadium) was the largest NFL stadium in the United States for three years, until the Detroit Lions' Pontiac Silverdome was built in 1975 (capacity: 80,325).

Cup o' Joe—According to National Public Radio, the first company to give its employees a coffee break was the Barcolo Manufacturing Co. in Buffalo in 1902 (later, the same company also gave the world the Barcalounger).

Where'd You Think It Came From?—The Christy Minstrels originated in Buffalo; naturally, one of their standards was, *Buffalo Girls.*

Nope, No Buffalos Here—There is no evidence that the buffalo ever inhabited the area around Buffalo. One theory is that early French explorers of the area came upon the Niagara River and named it "beau fleuve" ("beautiful river" in French), and that English-speaking settlers began to pronounce the name as "Buffalo." It's also possible an interpreter misconstrued the Indian word for "beaver" as "buffalo," since beaver abound in the area.

On Wings of Chicken—In 1964, Terressa Bellisimo deep-fried some leftover chicken wings, added some hot sauce, and served them to patrons of the Anchor Bar, her family's bar and restaurant at 1047 Main Street in Buffalo. Thus the spicy hors d'oeuvres Buffalo wings were born.

Oh, Gosh, Czolgosz—While President William McKinley was visiting the Temple of Music at the Pan-American Exposition in Buffalo on September 6, 1901, an anarchist named Leon Czolgosz ("zol-gosh") shot him. The president died at the home of John Milburg, at 1168 Delaware Avenue; his vice-president, Theodore Roosevelt, was inaugurated down the street at the home of his friend Ansley Wilcox, who lived at 641 Delaware Avenue.

Pip-Pip, Cheerios, and All That—The only place that General Mills manufactures Cheerios is its plant in Buffalo.

Ellenville
"It's not the end of the world, but you can see the end of the world from there." —DJ Ray Arthur

Freeport
"The stars first established summer homes at Freeport, and then the smalltimers precipitated a real-estate boom fighting to buy property and houses to make their home in Freeport to let the stars see how the other half lived." —comedian Fred Allen, in his autobiography *Much Ado About Me*

Great Neck
Where Gatsby Played—F. Scott Fitzgerald lived in Great Neck from 1922 to 1924, and used it as the model for West Egg, Long Island, where Jay Gatsby lived; the more affluent East Egg, where Daisy and Tom Buchanan lived, was based on Manhasset.

Ithaca

"Ithaca is a left winging, free thinking, grass rootsing, revolutionary community." —*www.virtualithaca.com*

Montauk

"Montauk Point—the eastern extremity of Long Island—is a region comparatively unknown, except to a few sportsmen, attracted thither by its very wildness, and to such tourists as find especial charms in its seclusion, and in the bold and picturesque scenery of its defiant promontory, upon which the wild Atlantic incessantly beats, and sometimes with tremendous violence. We had been informed that these tourists had a 'hard road to travel,' leading, after all, only to a 'wild, desolate country, infested by mosquitoes and snakes.'" —*Harper's New Monthly Magazine,* September 1871

"Montauk Point [is] where you stand on the rise by the lighthouse and look at the last tip of America below you, and on out toward Europe. Montauk Point is Carl Fisher's folly. It is a ghost town. The man who built the Indianapolis Speedway and who made Miami Beach had an idea about Montauk Point, but it didn't work." —journalist Ernie Pyle, July 6, 1936

Newburgh

Beginnings—New York was the first state to preserve an historic site when it commemorated George Washington's Revolutionary War headquarters at Newburgh.

New York City

"For some New Yorkers, gall isn't a flaw but a lifestyle choice, one of the seven habits of highly effective people." —Peggy Noonan, discussing Hillary Clinton's Senate campaign in the June 8, 1999, *Wall Street Journal*

"New York epitomizes the American city, Manhattan epitomizes New York, skyscrapers epitomize Manhattan, and the [World Trade Center] towers epitomize skyscrapers. Thus we have an Eastern grounding all the way down to ground zero." —William A. McClung, author of *Landscapes of Desire: Anglo Mythologies of Los Angeles*

"In the distance, the towers seem fragile. They rest so precisely on their vertical lines that the slightest shudder would knock them down like a house of cards. When the boat draws closer, their foundations seem firmer, but the

fall line remains indelibly traced. What a field day a bomber would have!"
—philosopher Simone de Beauvoir, January 26, 1947

"I'm in love with New York. [My husband] Frank says that what I love is not the real city, but the New York I built myself. That's true." —author Ayn Rand

"New York represented to [Ayn Rand] the pinnacle of human achievement in physical terms... The skyscrapers [represented] everything that man had traversed from the time of the cave to the time of his glorious and industrial civilization. That to her was what life was about—it wasn't just acquiring philosophy, it was acquiring ideas and acquiring science and then remaking the earth accordingly, and she couldn't think of a more splendid and exciting and beautiful place than that view you get of the skyscrapers where you don't see the details of each one but the mass of human ingenuity and talent soaring from the sky." —philosopher Leonard Peikoff

"I hate New York. Ten years away had dulled my memory of its inhuman tempo. I had forgotten what New York does to people's faces, how zoolike they look. I have forgotten the deafening crash of the elevateds, had forgotten that you can't walk a block without getting dust in your eyes, that people rush staringly along all day, bumping and dashing, and for what?" —journalist Ernie Pyle, August 14, 1935

"New York is no more America than Paris is France or London is England." —from John Steinbeck's *Travels with Charley*

"The beautiful metropolis of America is by no means so clean a city as Boston, but many of its streets have the same characteristics; except that the houses are not quite so fresh-coloured, the sign-boards are not quite so gaudy, the gilded letters not quite so golden, the bricks not quite so red, the stone not quite so white, the blinds and area railings not quite so green, the knobs and plates upon the street-doors not quite so bright and twinkling." —author Charles Dickens during his 1842 visit

"In a city that is so much a part of the global subconscious, it's pretty hard to pick a few highlights—wherever you go you'll feel like you've been there before." —*www.lonelyplanet.com*

"There are certain sections of New York, Major, that I'd advise you not to invade." —Humphrey Bogart as Rick Blaine in *Casablanca*

"If New Yorkers were asked to name the most important symbols of what has been widely celebrated as a glorious era for the city, they would probably start with the fact that the squeegee guys are off the streets." —Calvin Trillin in the July 14, 1997 *Time*

"New York City has become, once again, one of the most attractive tourist destinations in the world. Crime is plummeting at a historic rate. The national economic recovery is finally being felt there. Times Square, once dominated by pornography shops, is now the site of a Disney Store and theater. Yes, Gotham is now the Comeback Kid of U.S. cities." —Jesse Drucker in the November 1997 issue of *George*

"Let's get out of this company town and go to New York where no one cares what you are. Everybody's guilty of something in New York." —film director Abraham Polonsky to his wife, on escaping the Hollywood blacklist

"New York has a certain mythic quality as a city. It's the biggest of all American cities, and there's a certain sense of it being a self-contained, separate universe." —television producer Bill Finkelstein *(Brooklyn South, Civil Wars, L.A. Law)*

"It could only happen in Brooklyn. Nowhere else in this broad, untidy universe, not in Bedlam nor in Babel nor in the remotest psychopathic ward …only in the ancestral home of the Dodgers…could a man win a World Series by striking out." —Philadelphia Record sportswriter Red Smith, quoted in "The Play That Beat The Bums," October 20, 1997, *Sports Illustrated,* describing how a dropped third-strike ball sparked an eventual Yankee victory in the 1941 World Series

"The rest of the country looks upon New York like we're left-wing, Communist, Jewish, homosexual pornographers. I think of us that way sometimes, and I live here." —Woody Allen as Alvy Singer in *Annie Hall*

"People will kill each other for a parking space in New York because they think, 'If I don't get this one, I may never get a space. I'll be searching for months until somebody goes out to the Hamptons.' Because everybody in New York City knows there's way more cars than parking spaces. It's like musical chairs except everybody sat down around 1964." —Jerry Seinfeld in *Seinlanguage*

"There are roughly three New Yorks. There is, first, the New York of the man or woman who was born here, who takes the city for granted and accepts its size and its turbulence as natural and inevitable. Second, there is the New York of the commuter—the city that is devoured by locusts each day and spat out each night. Third, there is the New York of the person who was born somewhere else and came to New York in quest of something. Of these three trembling cities the greatest is the last—the city of final destination, the city that is a goal. It is this third city that accounts for New York's high-strung disposition, its poetical deportment, its dedication to the arts, and its incomparable achievements. Commuters give the city its tidal restlessness, natives give it solidity and continuity, but the settlers give it passion." —E.B. White in his essay "Here Is New York"

"Family visits to the Tennessee hills were once punctuated with questions such as, "Been mugged lately" and "Aren't you afraid to go out at night?" Gradually, this contemptuous line of inquiry has given way to a new enthusiastic curiosity—"Do you buy soup from the Soup Nazi?", everyone wants to know, or 'Have you been to the coffee shop where Jerry and his pals hang out?" New York is no longer a jungle to be feared; it's the place where you can relive last week's episode of *Seinfeld*. When out-of-towners are looking for office space in Manhattan they accept the notion that it's going to cost more than it would anywhere else. After all, Elaine shops for sponges here, Kramer drives Hansom cabs, and the cuddly cast of *Friends* works and hangs out in coffee houses that I can't find to save my life. It may not be possible to quantify, but the positive effect of "The *Seinfeld* Factor" can be summed up in one New York crime scene: Jerry stealing a loaf of rye bread from an old lady. With the *Seinfeld* crew at work, even a mugging looks good." —Collins Tuttle & Co. realtor Larry Nicks, spring 1996

"Yes, yes, I know; it's mean and ugly and rude and dirty and the traffic is a nightmare. No place is perfect. And yet, for the young and talented and ambitious, there's no place like it. It produces an electric energy like no other city in the world. It is the home of Broadway, Madison Avenue and Wall Street, streets that have come to symbolize entire industries. If you have the money and the energy, you can do something really interesting here every night of the week. Forever." —syndicated columnist Donald Kaul, in a June 23, 1996, column on livable cities

"I've always thought that if there were aliens, New York is where they'd feel most comfortable. I see people there all the time who I'm convinced must be aliens." —Barry Sonnenfeld, director of the alien-invasion movie *Men in Black*

"This guy is walking on Third Avenue and sees a man lying in the gutter. He rushes over and asks, 'Are you okay?' 'Sure,' the man says. 'I just found this parking space, and I sent my wife to buy a car.'" —author unknown

"If New York is a theme park, what is the theme? The city means many things to many people, but when you strip away all the cultural and economic differences that divide its inhabitants, there is a feeling almost all of them share, and it is essentially this: 'If one more taxi blocks my way at a busy intersection, I swear I am going to walk across its goddamned hood.'" —from "New York, The Ride," by Timothy K. Smith in the November 10, 1997, *Fortune*

"This is a very good land to fall in with and a pleasant land to see." —from Henry Hudson's journal entry of September 2, 1609, when the Half Moon anchored in lower New York

"Suddenly I found myself on Times Square. I had traveled eight thousand miles around the American continent and I was back on Times Square; and right in the middle of a rush hour, too, seeing with my innocent road-eyes the absolute madness and fantastic hoorair of New York with its millions and millions hustling forever for a buck among themselves, the mad dream—grabbing, taking, giving, sighing, dying, just so they could be buried in those author cemetery cities beyond Long Island City." —from Jack Kerouac's *On The Road*

"Tad's mission in life is to have more fun than anyone else in New York City, and this involves a lot of moving around, since there is always the likelihood that where you aren't is more fun than where you are. You are awed by his strict refusal to acknowledge any goal higher than the pursuit of pleasure. You want to be like that. You also think he is shallow and dangerous. His friends are all rich and spoiled, like the cousin from Memphis you met earlier in the evening who wouldn't accompany you below Fourteenth Street because, he said, he didn't have a lowlife visa." —from Jay McInerney's *Bright Lights, Big City*

Beginnings—Washington Irving first referred to New York as Gotham in his satirical essays, taking the name of the English city of Gotham, whose citizens reportedly avoided taxes by acting insane. Though Irving was suggesting the citizens of New York City were also somewhat insane, the negative connotations of the name eventually vanished.

Long Overdue—The RMS Titanic was scheduled to arrive at the Chelsea Piers on 23rd St. on April 16, 1912; the Carpathia, which rescued 675 of the 2,200 passengers aboard the doomed ocean liner, arrived at Chelsea Piers on April 20th.

Tallest Building—When the Woolworth Building was erected in New York City in 1913, it was the highest building in the world (792 feet) at the time.

The Bowery Boys—When the Dutch bought Manhattan Island in 1626, they designated six tracts of land and leased them for use as farms— the Dutch word for which is *bouwery.*

From the Interne: You Live In New York City When…
* You say "the city" and expect everyone to know you mean Manhattan.
* You have never been to the Statue of Liberty or the Empire State Building.
* You can get into a four-hour argument about how to get from Columbus Circle to Battery Park, but can't find Wisconsin on a map.
* You think Central Park is "nature."
* You believe that being able to swear at people in their own language makes you multi-lingual.
* You've worn out a car horn.
* You think eye contact is an act of aggression.

Niagara Falls

"It was not until I came on Table Rock, and looked—Great Heaven, on what a fall of bright green water!—that it came upon me in its full might and majesty. Then, when I felt how near to my Creator I was standing, the first effect, and the enduring one—instant and lasting—of the tremendous spectacle, was Peace." —author Charles Dickens during his 1842 visit

"The driver stops in front of a small building; there's a lunchroom, a souvenir shop, and an elevator that for fifty cents takes me down to water level. I look. What else is there to do? It's water. I go back up and we leave." —philosopher Simone de Beauvoir, February 19, 1947

"I'm very glad I saw it, because from now on if I am asked whether I have seen Niagara Falls I can say yes, and be telling the truth for once." — John Steinbeck, *Travels with Charley*

Peekskill

Beginnings—Actor Mel Gibson was born in Peekskill on January 3, 1956; a fan's Web site claims that his father moved the family to Australia in 1965 so that none of the five Gibson sons would have to serve in the Vietnam war, but after Gibson's Vietnam movie *We Were Soldiers* debuted, Gibson publicly disputed that story.

Rockville Centre

Money Dispensers—The first ATM was installed in Rockville Centre in 1969 by Chemical Bank.

Saratoga Springs

"The fountains of Saratoga will ever be the resort of wealth, intelligence, and fashion. As a political observatory no place can be more fitly selected. Gentleman are continually coming from and going to every section of the country; information from all quarters is received daily; and it is the best of all places for politicians to congregate. The great "combination" of opposite parties and opposing interests, by which General Jackson, Mr. Eaton, and Mr. Van Buren were brought into power, and John Quincy Adams turned out, was chiefly formed here; and it was here that the old Clintonians were sold out to "Jackson and Co." Saratoga, too, for a series of years, was the head-quarters of the "Albany Regency," under the leadership of Edwin Croswell and John Cramer—a combination which has never been equaled in its influence over the political destinies of New York State, and, though it, upon the nation." —*Harper's New Monthly Magazine,* 1876

"To get to Saratoga Springs, turn left on Union Avenue, and go back a hundred years." —*New York Times* sportswriter Red Smith

Beginnings—Potato chips were invented and first served at Moon's Lake House in Saratoga Springs.

Syracuse

"It would make an owl weep to fly over it." —unnamed New York City journalist, 1820

"The change seemed like one of enchantment." —the same journalist, returning in 1840

Keys to Better Typing—In 1903, Lyman C. Smith, a shotgun manufacturer, opened a factory at 701 E. Washington St. in Syracuse to manufacture typewriters. In 1926, his company merged with Corona Typewriter Co. of nearby Groton, which had developed the first portable typewriter. The resulting company, Smith-Corona, thrived until computers became popular; it went bankrupt in 1995.

The Oldest North American Government—On the shores of Onondaga Lake at least 500 years ago, near what is now Syracuse's Carousel Center mall, five Native American tribes met to create a union. The Senecas, Mohawks, Cayugas, Onondagas, and Oneidas created what became known as the Iroquois Confederacy. The importance of their agreement might have been lost to history, except that the tenets of how the tribes would be governed became the prototype for the U.S. Constitution.

Tuxedo Park

A Princely Fashion—A resident of Tuxedo Park named James Porter Brown dined with the Prince of Wales in the late 19th century. On that occasion, the prince (who later became King Edward VII) wore a black coat much shorter than a tailcoat. When Brown went back to his village in New York, he asked his tailor to recreate the fashion. The result was named the tuxedo.

Utica

Beginnings—Frank Winfield Woolworth opened his first five-and-ten store in Utica in 1879. It failed, and he tried again the same year in Lancaster, Penn., and was more successful.

North Carolina

Chapel Hill

"If God isn't a Tarheel, why is the sky Carolina blue?" —rhetorical question from University of North Carolina rooters

"Some folks in Chapel Hill are still trying to figure out which came first—the color of the sky or the color of the uniforms worn by North Carolina's athletes. In showing their devotion to those athletes, locals heed a simple rule of decor: If it ain't painted sky blue, it ain't painted." —Seth Davis in "The Top 50 Jock Schools," April 28, 1997, *Sports Illustrated*

Charlotte

"People here are probably never shirtless unless the lights are out." — Tom Sorensen, *Charlotte Observer* columnist, remarking on the fact that the buttoned-down crowd attending Panthers games cannot legally remove their shirts at Ericsson Stadium

On our behalf in June 2002, WSSS 104.7 DJ Sander Walker asked his listeners to describe Charlotte; among the responses:

"Where the three R's are racing, religion and 'restling!"
"Where proper English is a foreign language."
"You'll never feel like an outsider here because no one's from here."
"Under construction—come back for our grand opening."
"The only town where you can be at the corner of Queens, Queens, Queens and Queens and still be lost."

Greensboro

Beginnings—On February 1, 1960, four black college students sat down at the lunch counter of Woolworth's at the corner of Sycamore and Elm in Greensboro and refused to move, even after being told the lunch counter didn't serve food to "Negroes." The civil disobedience sit-in was born.

North Dakota

Quips & Quirks

"The Greater North Dakota Association, the state's chamber of commerce, is backing a proposal to cut the state's name to just Dakota. The organization says losing the 'North' would change people's perception of the state from a frigid treeless prairie to a frigid, treeless prairie that sounds like a stripper." —comedian Jon Stewart

"People have such an instant thing about how North Dakota is cold and snowy and flat." —former governor Ed Schafer, during a campaign to drop the word "north" from the state's name

"Well, you can put in a pig in a dress, but it wouldn't change the fact that it's a pig." —South Dakota state Rep. Mel Olson on the North Dakota plan to become "Dakota"

"North Dakota can reverse its reputation in one swoop by seceding from the U.S. to become Canada's balmiest province." —source unknown

"I never would have been president if not for my experiences in North Dakota." —Theodore Roosevelt, who ranched in the North Dakota Badlands from 1883 to 1886

"Rand McNally once accidentally left it out of its road atlas and it took a few weeks for anyone to notice." —travel writer and native Debora Halpern Wenger, in the December 2, 2001, *Tampa Tribune*

"With [the Theodore Roosevelt Rough Rider Award], the state honors North Dakotans who have done something prominent but not notorious, people such as Lawrence Welk and Roger Maris. As a former secretary of State, I just made the 'not notorious' cut." —Warren Christopher, writing in the August 3, 1998, *USA Today*

"Nothing was ever lost through enduring love of North Dakota." —graffiti on the side of a building in Sheyenne, N.D., cited by author Larry McMurtry, *Roads: Driving America's Great Highways*

Bismarck

"On the Bismarck side it is the Eastern landscape, Eastern grass, with the look and smell of Eastern America. Across the Missouri on the Mandan side, it is pure West, with brown grass and water scorings and small outcrops. The two sides of the river might well be a thousand miles apart." —John Steinbeck, *Travels with Charley*

Fargo

"If you will take a map of the United States and fold it in the middle, eastern edge against western, and crease it sharply, right in the crease will be Fargo." —John Steinbeck, *Travels with Charley*

Final Destination—When Buddy Holly, Richie Valens, and the Big Bopper died in an airplane crash on February 3, 1959, their destination was Fargo.

Grand Forks

"I arrived at Grand Forks International Airport on a sub-zero Tuesday night. I have never been so cold in my life. And that was inside the terminal. Outside it was much worse... The way North Dakotans deal with this is to leave their cars running... [N]obody steals the unattended cars, or anything else. During my visit, roughly once every four minutes a North Dakotan would remind me, in a nice way, that they have hardly any crime up there, in contrast to my city, Miami, where, as the North Dakotans understand it, you can't hear yourself think for all the machine-gun fire." —humorist Dave Barry, who visited Grand Forks after the city had named a sewage treatment plant after him.

Rugby

Middle of the Road—While the geographical center of the all 50 states is in South Dakota, Rugby is the geographical center of North America.

Ohio

Quips & Quirks

"Ohio could, without becoming more densely populated than many provinces of Europe, have ten million inhabitants. The fertility of the country seems inexhaustible. It is wonderfully watered by three or four little streams, tributaries of the Ohio, which run back towards the Great Lakes."—Alexis de Tocqueville, December 2, 1831; the philosopher was prescient—in the 2000 census, Ohio's population was 11,353,140

"In Boston, in New York, in Philadelphia, there is already a class which has acquired property and which has adopted sedentary habits and wants to enjoy wealth, not to make it. In Ohio, everyone has come to make money. No one has been born there; no one wants to stay there; there is not a *single*, absolutely not a *single* man of leisure, not a single speculative mind. Everyone has his work, to which he devotes himself ardently." —Alexis de Tocqueville, December 2, 1831

Presidential Beginnings—18th president Ulysses S. Grant, born in Point Pleasant on April 27, 1822, was the first of seven natives Ohio sent to the White House (Grant, Garfield, Hayes, Benjamin Harrison, McKinley, Taft, and Harding) in a span of 52 years between 1869 and 1921; this is second only to Virginia, which sent eight natives to the White House (Washington, Jefferson, Madison, Monroe, William Henry Harrison, Tyler, Taylor, Wilson), seven within the span of 60 years from 1789 to 1849.

Akron
"There is about the city the turbulent and impatient manner of a miracle town, with all the symptoms of a community that has grown fast and does not want to stop growing. In the shops, in the restaurants, and along Main Street, people move fast, eat fast, talk fast. It is as if the boom that rubber brought to town 30 years ago had subsided in the factories only, and still agitated the townspeople." —*The Ohio Guide*, published by the Works Progress Administration, 1940

Canton
"Canton people love to go to market. Almost every day, and especially on Saturday, even the most sedate men in the city, the professional, business, and political leaders, may be seen shopping for groceries, meats, and other home things. This and many another aspect of the city, such as its neatness,

make Canton seem younger than it is, as if it were not old enough to understand that a large steel city is supposed to be burly and hard and overgrown." —from *The Ohio Guide*, published by the Works Progress Administration, 1940

Cincinnati

"Cincinnati presents an odd spectacle. A town which seems to want to get built too quickly to have things done in order. Large buildings, huts, streets blocked by rubble, houses under construction; no names to the streets, no numbers on the houses, no external luxury, but a picture of industry and work that strikes one at every step." —Alexis de Tocqueville, December 4, 1831

"As long as Marge Schott's not your neighbor, Cincinnati is a friendly, kids-in-the-front-yard kind of place." —Geoffrey Precourt and Anne Faircloth in "Best Cities: Where the Living Is Easy," November 11, 1996, *Fortune*

"Say Cincinnati to an outlander and he will probably reply, with almost a reflect action, 'beer and Germans.'" —*The Ohio Guide*, published by the Works Progress Administration, 1940

"Cincinnati is a beautiful city; cheerful, thriving, and animated. I have not often seen a place that commends itself so favourably and pleasantly to a stranger at the first glance as this does: with its clean houses of red and white, its well-paved roads, and footways bright tile. Nor does it become less prepossessing on a closer acquaintance. The streets are broad and airy, the shops extremely good, the private residences remarkable for their elegance and neatness." —author Charles Dickens, during his 1842 visit

"There is no major lure unless you count cheerful typicality— sociologists have ranked Cincinnati one of the nation's most 'typical' cities, by whatever statistical or demographic measure." —*www.lonelyplanet.com*

Uncle Tom's Cabin Inspiration—Harriet Beecher Stowe was reputedly inspired to write Uncle Tom's Cabin after she read an abolitionist pamphlet written by a professor at Cincinnati's Presbyterian Lane Seminary; the famous scene in which Eliza crosses the ice floes recreated an actual crossing by a fugitive slave over the Ohio River (although several other towns along the Ohio claim she actually crossed *there*).

Once The Center—In the 1870 census, the center of the U.S. population was just outside Cincinnati.

Deal—Cincinnati is the world's largest producer of playing cards.

Batter Up—In 1876, the Cincinnati Red Stockings were the first professional baseball team.

Price Check—The first UPC code-based scanning system was installed at a Kroger grocery store in Cincinnati in 1967.

Cleveland

"Ohio's [state motto] is 'With God, all things are possible.' But no one there has yet bought my proposed addition to that: '...whereas with Cleveland, who knows?'" —humorist Bill Tammeus in the February 2, 1996, *Kansas City Star*

"People in New York and Los Angeles want to have careers. People in Cleveland are happy to have jobs. I think more of America is like Cleveland." —Bruce Helford, producer of *The Drew Carey Show*

"Like its comic embodiment, Drew Carey, Cleveland is a city that behaves like a schlub but underneath is strangely appealing. The city once known as the 'Mistake on the Lake' is making a comeback." —*Forbes* writer David Dukcevich

The Running Begins—The story that became *The Fugitive* was inspired by a Cleveland case in 1954 in which osteopath Sam Sheppard was convicted of killing his wife.

Beginnings—The city of Cleveland was founded by Moses Cleaveland, who originally mapped it. The spelling changed, according to legend, when on July 1, 1832, the compositor of new and garrulously titled *Cleveland Gazette and Commercial Register* ran out of space on his masthead and dropped the first 'a' in Cleaveland, a simplification that caught on.

Presidential Endings—20th president James Garfield is buried in Cleveland's Lake View Cemetery.

Beginnings—Actors Paul Newman (January 26, 1925) and Halle Berry (August 14, 1968) were born in Cleveland (Berry was reputedly named for the Halle Brothers department store).

Columbus

"In the early days of the nineteenth century, Columbus won out, as state capital, by one vote over Lancaster, and ever since then has had the hallucination that it is being followed, a curious municipal state of mind which affects, in some way or other, all those who live there." —James Thurber, "More Alarms At Night"

"Buckeyes football isn't a matter of life and death in Columbus—it's much more important than that." —from a profile of Ohio State football coach John Cooper, September 8, 1997, *Sports Illustrated*

"Columbus in terms of its people rather than its buildings is three cities in one. In the low, gray stone capitol in its 10-acre square, and in the mobile 'little capitol' that moves from one smoke-filled room to another in the hotels across High Street, the political city has its life... The educational city centers on the Ohio State University... The third intramural city, quite distinct from the other two and less compact, is one of varied commerce and industry. It is visibly symbolized in the lofty American Insurance Union Citadel, and in the smoking stacks of foundries and shops scattered about town, where several hundred plants make products ranging from violins to steel railroad cars." —from *The Ohio Guide,* published by the Works Progress Administration, 1940

Irony Filings—William Sydney Porter, under the pseudonym O. Henry, wrote many of his short stories while confined in the Ohio State Penitentiary at 248 W. Spring St. in Columbus.

Hamburger Heaven—The first White Castle hamburger restaurant opened in Columbus in 1929 at 49 S. Front St., while Dave Thomas established the first of its Wendy's hamburger restaurants at 257 E. Broad St. in 1969.

First of a Kind Schools—German settlers established America's first kindergartens in Columbus in 1858, while the first junior high school, Indianola Junior High School (now Indianola Middle School), opened on September 7, 1909, at 420 E. 19th Ave. .

First Drive-Up Bank—On June 5, 1950, Bank One opened the first drive-up teller window at its branch at the corner of Olentangy River Rd. and Third Ave. in Columbus.

Dayton

"The very nature of the Dayton economy has attracted a high type of workman and artisan, and drawn men and women of culture and skill to the city. The effect is marked not only in the physical appearance of Dayton, but also in the tone and quality of its social and civic life." —*The Ohio Guide,* published by the Works Progress Administration, 1940

Big Business—A mechanic named Charles Kettering came to Dayton in 1906 to work at the National Cash Register Co. (better known today as computer manufacturer NCR). He quit this job in 1909 to fashion what became a self-starter for automobiles; a year later he bagged a big order for none other than Cadillac, and with a partner he incorporated the Dayton Engineering Laboratories Company (eventually known as the General Motors division called Delco). It was Kettering who, with General Motors chairman Alfred P. Sloan, established New York's Sloan-Kettering Hospital.

East Liverpool

Gangster Shootout—On October 22, 1934, Chicago G-man Melvin Purvis led a group of federal agents and East Liverpool police to a farm to capture outlaw Charles "Pretty Boy" Floyd. When Floyd refused to surrender and sprinted toward a shed, pistols and machine guns let loose and the bank robber died of his wounds 15 minutes later.

Marietta

"No colony in America was ever settled under such favorable auspices as that which has just commenced on the banks of the Muskingum... I know many of the settlers personally and there never were men better calculated to promote the welfare of a community." —George Washington

Oberlin

Beginnings—In December of 1833, Oberlin became the first college to admit women.

Put-in-Bay

During the war of 1812, Commodore Oliver Hazard Perry, badly outnumbered, fought the British near this Lake Erie port. Upon vanquishing the British, Perry sent the famous message, "We have met the enemy and they are ours."

"Put-in-Bay lives off wine and summer excursions. It is a town in faded glory. Once it was a place of great exclusive hotels. Now it is bait for thousands of city excursionists who come for the ride and two hours of loud music." —journalist Ernie Pyle, July 26, 1938

Sandusky
"Sandusky was something like the back of an English watering-place, out of the season." —author Charles Dickens during his 1842 visit

Toledo
"The inhabitants chose the name Toledo, but the reason for this choice is buried in a welter of legends… Whatever the origin, it eventually resulted in a peculiar rapprochement with the Spanish city of the same name. The city's oldest newspaper is named the Toledo Blade and was awarded the royal coat of arms by the Spanish Government. In 1931, the University of the City of Toledo was granted permission to use the arms of Ferdinand and Isabella as its motif, and three years later a goodwill delegation of local citizens returned from the Spanish city burdened with gifts for the museum of art and the new cathedral." —*The Ohio Guide,* published by the Works Progress Administration, 1940

And Still Counting—The highest numbered street in the United States is Toledo's 326th Street.

Youngstown
"From the city square, on nights when production is up and the mills are roaring, the horizon is painted with an uncertain light where the stack-flung ceiling of smoke gives back the glare of the mill fires. And when production is down and only a few furnaces carry 'heats,' the forlornness of the squat and silent mills seeps out into the whole city." —*The Ohio Guide,* published by the Works Progress Administration, 1940

Oklahoma

Quips & Quirks

"The Oklahoma panhandle, which I cross in 45 minutes, is still as lonely, lovely, and spooky as ever. There is some farming, but it is still mainly an area of ranches, inhabited by hardy souls who like to be left alone to fend for themselves." —author Larry McMurtry, *Roads: Driving America's Great Highways*

Oklahoma City

"Oklahoma City is an especially friendly town. People there have a pride about their town—not a silly civic pride, but that same feeling that exists in San Francisco and New Orleans. They just wouldn't live anywhere else, that's all." —journalist Ernie Pyle

"You top a little rise, and the fog of lights divides slowly into individualities. You see tall buildings all lighted up, still far away. You think what a big place Oklahoma City is, with lots of big office buildings—and lots of people working this late at night, too. Why it looks like the New York skyline at night, only the buildings all seem about the same height... And then suddenly it hits you, right between the eyes. Those aren't buildings all lighted up. They're oil derricks! Oil derricks right in the city." —journalist Ernie Pyle, June 9, 1936

"It is a community born of and sustained by oil—at one time oil derricks crowded so close to the state capitol that an arcade of wooden awnings had to be constructed to keep the legislators from being splattered on their way to work." —author Larry McMurtry, *Roads: Driving America's Great Highways*

Food Stuff—The shopping cart was invented by Sylvan Goldman in Oklahoma City in 1937. It enabled shoppers to buy more groceries and thus inspired the growth of supermarkets.

No Dome—Construction of the state capitol suffered from not only cost overruns but also material shortages caused by World War I. Although it was originally supposed to have a dome, the idea was scrapped and today it's one of the few capitol buildings without one.

Tulsa

Road Stuff—The first *yield* sign in the United States was posted at Tulsa's most dangerous intersection in 1950. Reading "Yield Right-of-Way," it reduced accidents enough to drop the intersection to seventh on the list of most dangerous.

Oregon

Quips & Quirks

So That's Where It Came From—During World War II, a group of counties in southern Oregon and northern California attempted to secede and form the state of Jefferson in order to get better federal funding. The effort was short-lived, but the idea of what its air force would be named was incarnated in the rock group Jefferson Airplane.

From the Internet: You Live in Oregon When...
- Your idea of a traffic jam is 10 cars waiting to pass a tractor on the highway.
- "Vacation" means going to Portland for the weekend.
- You measure distance in hours.
- You know several people who have hit deer more than once.
- You often switch from "heat" to "a/c" in the same day.
- You use a down comforter in the summer.
- Your grandparents drive 65 mph through 2 feet of water during a raging rainstorm without flinching.
- You see people wearing hunting clothes at social events.
- You install security lights on your house and garage and leave both unlocked.
- You think of the major food groups as elk meat, beer, fish, and berries.
- You carry jumper cables in your car and your wife knows how to use them.
- There are seven empty cars running in the parking lot at the BiMart store at any given time.
- You design your kid's Halloween costume to fit under a raincoat.
- Driving is better in the winter because almost everybody stays home.
- You think sexy lingerie is tube socks and flannel pajamas.
- You know all the important seasons: almost winter, winter, still raining, road construction, deer season, and elk season.
- It takes you three hours to go to the store for one item even when you're in a rush because you have to stop and talk to everyone in town.
- You actually understand these jokes and forward them to all your friends in Oregon or those who used to live here.

Portland

"In New York, people live to work and in Portland, people work to live. Five o'clock rolls around in Portland and people actually leave work to go out and hike, bike, fish, or just enjoy themselves outdoors." —Jeff Wallach, former New Yorker, quoted in "The 10 Best Places to Live," July 1996 *Swing*

"Last spring, I went to Portland, Oregon, and fell in love. Just flying in—over fir-topped mountains—was a treat. The air smelled fresh and clean and sweet, and the city itself, where you can look up and see green from every street corner, was a marvel." —editor Ruth Reichl, writing in the January 2002 *Gourmet*

"Everybody here is crazy about Portland. They rave about it. They don't talk Chamber of Commerce folders; they don't talk about their industries and their schools and their crops. They roar about what a wonderful place Portland is to just live in. People do live well here. This whole Northwest country is beautiful, and the climate is pleasant, and existence is gentle." —journalist Ernie Pyle, October 29, 1936

"The Pearl District is reminiscent of New York's SoHo before the chain stores moved in—although, like everything in Portland, it's far cleaner." —unnamed editor in the January 2002 *Travel & Leisure*

"Portland may not be the biggest, fastest or most dazzling metropolis on Earth, but it's got to be one of the most appealing. [It] is a city of greenery and grace notes." —writer David Armstrong, in the June 3, 2001, *San Francisco Chronicle*

"Portland is a bracing mixture—vital without being precocious, laid-back without being starry-eyed... More than that, Portland is funky. Not in a self-conscious way, but as a reflection of how the locals choose to live." —*The London Times* [get original citation]

Small and Large—Portland is the home of both the world's smallest park (24-inch Mill Ends Park) and the nation's largest forested city wilderness (5,000-acre Forest Park).

The Statue of Liberty is First—"Portlandia" in front of the Portland Building is the second largest copper statue in the U.S.

Salem

Massachusetts West—The name of the capital city was decided by the flip of a coin; the other choice was Boston.

Pennsylvania

Quips & Quirks

Indiana

Beginnings—Actor James Stewart was born in his parents' home on Philadelphia Street in Indiana on May 20, 1908; for years his father kept the actor's Oscar for *The Philadelphia Story* in his hardware store window.

Philadelphia

"It is a handsome city, but distractingly regular. After walking about it for an hour or two, I felt that I would have given the world for a crooked street. The collar of my coat appeared to stiffen, and the brim of my hat to expand, beneath its Quaker influence." —author Charles Dickens during his 1842 visit

"The most conservative city in America." —Charles Francis Adams during an 1860 campaign speech for Abraham Lincoln's presidential bid

"The streets are safe in Philadelphia—it's only the people who make them unsafe." —Mayor Frank Rizzo

"The city itself was voted the country's friendliest. And still, despite the support of rah-rah patriots and the cappuccino crowd, the 'City of Brotherly Love' has long been the butt of jokes by W.C. Fields and lesser-known detractors. When the insults finally soaked in—just in time for America's bicentennial in 1976—the city began renovating its many historical buildings and cultural institutions. The soon-to-follow *Rocky* films further bolstered Philly's oversentimental sense of American self-reliance, graduating from the Ben Franklin fraternity of rebellious Constitutionaries to the muscled bravado of a monosyllabic boxer. Ah, America, land of contrasts." —*www.lonelyplanet.com*

Only Two Inaugural Balls—The only two presidents inaugurated in Philadelphia were George Washington and John Adams.

Sticky Business—Walter Diemer was an accountant for Fleer, the Philadelphia chewing gum manufacturer, in 1928, when he came up with the idea for bubble gum. When he cooked up a five-pound batch and test-marketed it in a Philadelphia grocery store, it sold out in an afternoon. Diemer had to teach the Fleer salesmen how to blow bubbles so they could demonstrate the product.

Pittsburgh

"What makes Pittsburgh such an inviting place are things hidden in all the hills and valleys that reach out from the banks of the three rivers. The topography long ago encouraged separated neighborhoods to form, and that same topography now discourages these neighborhoods from meshing into one homogenized mass." —travel writer Jeanne Marie Laskas

"Pittsburgh is undoubtedly the cockeyedest city in the United States. Physically, it is absolutely irrational. It must have been laid out by a mountain goat... The reason for all this is the topography of Pittsburgh. It's up and down, and around and around, and in betwixt. Pittsburgh is hills, mountains, cliffs, valleys, and rivers. Some streets are narrow; some are wide. None runs more than a few blocks in a straight line." —journalist Ernie Pyle, April 16, 1937

"If they knew what they liked, they wouldn't live in Pittsburgh." —Joel McCrea as film director John L. Sullivan in *Sullivan's Travels*

And the Raiders Are Still Upset—Three Rivers Stadium in Pittsburgh was the site of football's famous Immaculate Reception play on December 23, 1972, when Steelers quarterback Terry Bradshaw, on a fourth-and-ten-yards play with 22 seconds left to play, threw a desperation pass to running back Frenchy Fuqua. The ball bounced off the shoulder pads of Oakland Raiders defensive back Jack Tatum and into the arms of running back Franco Harris, who took it 60 yards for the winning touchdown.

Titusville

More Sticky Business—E.L. Drake discovered oil in Titusville in 1859, inaugurating the beginnings of the U.S. oil industry.

Valley Forge

"Through parks, hills, and green valleys, on little twisting, overgrown roads, I'm driven to the famous site of Valley Forge. This is where, after losing Philadelphia, Washington camped through a long winter with a handful of men, whom cold and hungered claimed day after day; he dreaded an attack that would easily have annihilated his forces. No one knows by what miracle the English general passed up his chance and remained entrenched in Philadelphia like Hannibal at Capua." —philosopher Simone de Beauvoir, April 24, 1947

Rhode Island

Quips & Quirks

"In respect to scenic and recreational details, chief emphasis has been placed upon the coastal regions rather than the relatively uninteresting and sparsely populated inland area." —from the preface to the Federal Writers' Project's *Rhode Island: A Guide to the Smallest State* (1937)

"They say that in the world there's six degrees of separation. In Rhode Island, it's more like one and a half degrees." —State Attorney General Patrick Lynch, February, 2003

Big and Small—Rhode Island may be the smallest state, but it has the longest name. Though it's only 1084 square miles, its borders were not firmly established until the 19th century (the northern boundary in 1883, the western boundary in 1887, and the eastern boundary in 1899).

And the Island You Rhode In On—When Italian navigator Verrazano (for whom New York's Verrazano Bridge is named) sailed in Narragansett Bay, he was reminded of the Greek island of Rhodes—probably by present day Block Island. The name stuck.

Harrisville

"Harrisville is so remote, its zip code is 00000." —Joe Webb, printing analyst whose business address is Harrisville

Newport

"There are three distinct Newports: the first is the blunt old center, now partly dependent on the army and navy bases and the summer resort; the second is the military and naval Newport, which lives on its own reservations; and the third is the opulent resort Newport behind and below the old center. Each of the three Newports ignores the others." —*Rhode Island: A Guide to the Smallest State*, Federal Writers' Project, 1937

Oldest Synagogue—The Touro Synagogue was built in 1763, making it the oldest surviving synagogue in North America.

Beginnings—Matthew Perry, younger brother of Oliver Hazard Perry, opened U.S. relations with Japan in 1854, and was born in Newport. Also born in Newport was Gilbert Stuart, whose portrait of George Washington graces the $1 bill (he did some 124 portraits of the first president). Ironically, Stuart was a Tory sympathizer who left the U.S. when the Revolutionary War broke out and only returned in 1792 because he was in debt.

Jack & Jackie Marry—John F. Kennedy and Jacqueline Bouvier were married at St. Mary's Church; the reception was held at Hammersmith Farm, home of the bride's mother and stepfather.

South Carolina

Quips & Quirks

Charleston

"When you come in [via Greyhound bus], however, you get only as far as North Charleston—a chance to see the sprawling, modern, scruffy, fast-food town full of the poor and nearly poor who cannot afford the decorative, agreeable, goldfish-bowl of historic downtown Charleston itself." —travel writer Michael Gray in the September 11, 1999, *London Daily Telegraph*

"Being born in Charleston confers upon one more than an address. It's a birthright, an identity forged from this matrix of saltwater, palmettos and urban antiquity, inseparable from one's DNA—a complicated heritage, luminous and elegant, but also bloody and disaster-strewn. Charleston breeds a fierce devotion among its sons and daughters. In an age noted for transitoriness, Charlestonians stay put for generations, rooted, somehow, in this vortex of swift tidal rivers, light-stung marshes and deep languid shade. We have an intense pride of place, a conviction that, despite all the calamities that have befallen the city over the centuries, no other place on earth is quite so preferred by God." —*Charleston Post-Courier* columnist Barbara Hagerty, writing in the March 7, 1993, *Los Angeles Times Magazine*

"I'm going to Charleston. I want to see if somewhere there isn't something left in life of charm and grace." —Clark Gable as Rhett Butler in *Gone With the Wind*

"I've found that my out of town guests are beguiled more by Charleston's houses than by anything else. That's understandable, because our houses are flirts. Lined up along the streets, they are approachable and alluring, without the vast front lawns or privacy fencing with which suburban houses shield themselves. These houses are touchable, right from sidewalk, yet at the same time they are clearly private." —Josephine Humphreys in *Travel Holiday*

"Charleston is perhaps South Carolina's best kept secret—an impossibly beautiful old world town filled with flowering trees, cobblestone streets, pastel hued antebellum mansions and the traditions of a history redolent with romance and tragedy." —Robb Beattie in *Doctor's Review*

"For Charlestonians, Charleston is not so much a place as a calling. They are as devoted to their city as the Athenians are to Athens and Parisians to Paris. They may travel to foreign parts or even leave for years at a time, but they always dream of coming home." —unnamed editor in *Gourmet*

"There may be a more relaxing way to spend an afternoon than drowsing in a hammock on a Charleston piazza, listening to the clip clop of hoofs as horse drawn carriages roll by...then again, there may not." —travel writer Bill Spurr

The Northern War of Aggression Begins—Confederate soldiers in Fort Johnson fired on Fort Sumter at the mouth of Charleston harbor on April 12, 1861, which marked the beginning of the Civil War.

The Dance Started Here—The Roaring Twenties dance known as the Charleston was indeed created in Charleston, though it first gained notice in an all-black revue performing in New York. It was an easy dance because one could stand in one place and do it.

Fore-front—The first golf club in America was established in Charleston in 1876.

South Dakota

Quips & Quirks

"People in South Dakota used to wear T-shirts that said, 'We have two seasons, shovel and swat.'" —actress and Huron native Cheryl Ladd

"We're a very, very polite people who get uneasy in the midst of conflict." —South Dakota State University political science professor Bob Burns, commenting on the nasty 1996 Senate campaign between Republican Larry Pressler and Democrat Tim Johnson

"The grasshopper is to the Dakotas about the same thing as a hurricane is to Miami or a tidal wave is to Galveston." —journalist Ernie Pyle, July 20, 1936

Geographical Center—The geographical center of all 50 states (including Alaska) is approximately 45 degrees north and 104 degrees west, just a few miles east of where the borders of South Dakota, Wyoming, and Montana meet.

Badlands

"Hell with the fires burned out." —George Armstrong Custer

Black Hills

Them Thar Hills—In 1874, miners accompanying an army general and his regiment in the Black Hills discovered gold on Sioux land, inspiring the phrase, "There's gold in them thar hills." Little did they know—in fact, three miles west of Deadwood sat the largest gold mine in the western hemisphere, the Homestake Gold Mine (it was owned by George Hearst, father of publisher William Randolph Hearst). The gold rush also aggravated relations between the Army and the Sioux. In 1876, the Sioux attacked and annihilated the regiment of George Armstrong Custer—the general who'd led the miners into the hills two years before.

Deadwood

Third in Line—When it legalized gambling in 1989, Deadwood was the third city in the United States to do so, after Las Vegas and Atlantic City.

Tennessee

Quips & Quirks

"Nothing in Kentucky or Tennessee gives the impression of a finished society; in that respect these two States are essentially different from those newly peopled by the Americans of the North, in which one finds the germs of high civilization of New England. In Kentucky or Tennessee one sees few churches and no schools. Society, like the individuals, seems to foresee nothing." —Alexis de Tocqueville, December, 1831

"As far as Lusa could tell, the entire border of the state of Tennessee was ringed with shacks advertising cheap fireworks. It had to do with their being legal on one side of the line and not the other, but she wasn't sure which was which." —from Barbara Kingsolver's *Prodigal Summer*

More Neighbors—Tennessee and Missouri are the only states bordering on eight other states; their neighbor Kentucky borders on seven.

Chattanooga

Celebrating Battle—When it was established in 1890, Chickamauga-Chattanooga National Military Park was the first park commemorating a battle.

The Trail of Tears Begins—Cherokee Indians were forcibly banished from Chattanooga to Oklahoma in 1838, beginning the legendary Trail of Tears.

Dayton

"The town, I confess, greatly surprised me. I expected to find a squalid Southern village, with darkies snoozing on the horse blocks, pigs rooting under the houses and the inhabitants full of bookworm and malaria. What I found was a country town of charm and even beauty." —*Baltimore Sun* reporter H.L. Mencken, from his account of "The Monkey Trial"

Scopes Trial—In this small town (1920 pop. 1,800; 2000 pop. 6,180) in eastern Tennessee, about 36 miles from Chattanooga, in the spring of 1925, John Scopes dared to teach evolution to his high-school science class, prompting the legendary battle between William Jennings Bryan and Clarence Darrow portrayed in *Inherit The Wind.* (Tennessee did not abolish its anti-evolution law until 1968.) Nebraska native Bryan, a three-time democratic nominee for president, died there on July 26, 1925, five days after winning the conviction of Scopes (who was fined $100).

Eastport

"We live on a mountain and don't hear any sirens, planes or even cars passing by. When a car does go by and you're outside, everyone waves at you. This was strange to me at first." —Lorraine Vener, a Silicon Valley transplant

Memphis

"If Beale Street could talk, married men would take their babes and walk." —composer W.C. Handy

"In its turn-of-the-century heyday, Beale Street was the hub of social, civic and business activity for the city's large African-American community and much of the middle South. Today, the Disneyfication of the two-block strip of Beale between 2nd and 4th Streets might give some travelers the blues. The rough and tumble barrooms and brothels of yore have been replaced by swanky clubs, restaurants, souvenir shops and neon signs— something of a blues theme park." —*www.lonelyplanet.com*

"Memphis possesses a jagged vitality that seems more western than southern, as if its inhabitants have never been told that the frontier has moved on and, finally, disappeared. Although physically situated in Tennessee it is the spiritual capital of Mississippi, the metropolis to which planters sent their wives for finery and their sons for dissipation; and to which the sons and daughters of their slaves migrated to escape the brutal drudgery of the cotton fields. The city was once abandoned to fever, and a riverine funk still hangs over the housing projects of the South Side as well as the mansions to the east. At least that's one theory, that it is the big river that makes people there a little crazy—the car-crashing debutantes, the love-triangle murderers, the dipsomaniacal aunts, the suicide uncles, Elvis." —Jay McInerney in his novel *The Last of the Savages*

Nashville

"If I am ever so fortunate as to reach the Pearly Gates of the New Jerusalem I shall expect to find nothing more radiantly beautiful than the Parthenon at Nashville at night." —unknown newspaper reporter after the opening of the city's replica of the Athens Parthenon in 1951

"Many of Nashville's drivers could fairly be said to be living in their own heads. Though a large, sophisticated city now, Nashville still seems to me to be dominated by the suspicious us-and-them psychology of the mountain hollows; Appalachian passivity alternates unpredictably with Appalachian ferocity." —author Larry McMurtry, *Roads: Driving America's Great Highways*

"Nashville is a surprise—a complex personality best described as a Janus, a two-sided phenomenon that brings delights to visitors and residents alike. The 'Music City' side is bold and loud and comes first to mind—a Johnny-come-lately with obvious flash and dash. *Nashville's* quieter side reflects her nineteenth-century role as a cultural and historical center, but with plenty of charms to interest twenty-first-century visitors. The lady is just a bit too genteel to toot her own horn loudly. Put the two sides together and you've got yin and yang and one terrific combination. —Susann Tepperberg, May 2001 *Physicians' Travel & Meeting Guide*

"Nashville occupies that nebulous southeastern region between Middle America, the East Coast, 'Down South,' and 'Up North.' It's decidedly southern in most aspects but so close to the other regions that the distinction sometimes gets blurred. At any rate, whether it's because the U.S. is moving towards the South or the South is moving towards the rest of the country, Nashville seems more than ever like an all-American city—and one of the most guileless you're ever likely to visit." —*www.lonelyplanet.com*

The Right to Vote—On August 18, 1920, in the Tennessee House of Representatives in Nashville, the youngest member of the legislature, 23-year-old Republican Harry Thomas Burn crossed party lines and broke a tie in the vote to approve the 19th amendment to the constitution. As a result, Tennessee became the 36th state—and last necessary—to ratify the amendment to give women the right to vote.

Newport
"Back in prohibition days, hundreds of stills were hidden around the mountain slopes [of Cocke County]. The agents sometimes captured as many as thirty stills and seventy-five men in one day. Moonshine was selling for twenty dollars a gallon... But the old days are gone. Repeal, and the new [Great Smoky] national park, and tighter restrictions on moonshiners' supplies, have pretty well shot the business." —journalist Ernie Pyle, October 15, 1940

Texas

Quips & Quirks

A Texas Joke—A Texan was changing planes in New York City and decided to call a friend in New Jersey. He dialed the number and the operator informed him it would cost three dollars for the first three minutes. "Three dollars?" he raged. "Why, back home in Texas I can call to hell and back for three dollars!" Replied the operator, "Yes, sir, but in Texas, that would be a local call."

"A Texan outside of Texas is a foreigner... Outside their state I think Texans are a little frightened and very tender in their feelings, and these qualities cause boasting, arrogance, and noisy complacency—the outlets of shy children. At home Texans are none of these things. The ones I know are gracious, friendly, generous, and quiet. In New York we hear them so often bring up their treasured uniqueness. Texas is the only state that came into the Union by treaty. It retains the right to secede at will. We have heard them threaten to secede so often that I formed an enthusiastic organization—The American Friends for Texas Secession. This stops the subject cold. They want to be able to secede but they don't want anyone to want them to." —John Steinbeck, *Travels with Charley*

"If I owned both hell and Texas, I'd rent out Texas and live in hell." — General Philip Sheridan

"No one is a true Texan who uses 'summer' as a verb." —columnist Molly Ivins (specifically referring to Houston transplant and 39th president George Bush)

"Politics, particularly in Texas, is great entertainment—better than the zoo, better than the circus, rougher than football, and even more aesthetically satisfying than baseball." —columnist Molly Ivins

"The pleasant stretch of prairie that once lay between Austin and San Antonio has been filled in with San Marcos, New Braunfels, a large outlet mall, and a racetrack. This is what one might call urban scatter, since it lacks the full density of urban sprawl." —author Larry McMurtry, *Roads: Driving America's Great Highways*

First Female Governor—On November 4, 1924, Texas elected the first female governor in the United States, Miriam Ferguson; she ran to vindicate her husband, James F. Ferguson, who had been impeached from the governor's office seven years before on charges of financial malfeasance.

Archer City

"We were thoroughly landlocked. I had no river to float on, to wonder about. Highway 281 was my river, its hidden reaches a mystery and an enticement." —author Larry McMurtry, *Roads;* McMurtry's novel *The Last Picture Show* took place in a fictional representation of Archer City

Arlington

"[It's] not so much of a city as an area of confusion that manages to combine the worst features of Dallas (just to the east) and Fort Worth (just to the west)." —author Larry McMurtry, *Roads: Driving America's Great Highways*

Athens

Although as many as four towns claim to be the birthplace of the hamburger, food writer Renee Klentz cites Athens resident Fletcher Davis as the man who put fried ground beef on bread with onion, pickles, and mustard, sometime in the 1880s.

Austin

"If you grew up anywhere in Texas and were kind of different, Austin would be the kind of place you'd gravitate to." —film director Richard Linklater, quoted in *Fortune,* November 23, 1998

"Austin has always been the sort of town where the '60s never really died, where creativity was encouraged and free spirits were nurtured." — Anne Faircloth, writing in *Fortune,* November 23, 1998

"Visiting Austin is like living in a song-a folk-punk-rockabilly-country-blues-tune so audacious it stomps around inside your head for months. You can't be bored in Austin. The city and the surrounding scenic Hill Country have more energy, optimism, good food, and things to do than most areas can even dream of offering. It's truly the heart of Texas." — *www.bestfares.com*

"What's so special about [the Congress Ave. Bridge]? Bats! The bridge's 1980 reconstruction created crevices beneath the bridge that somehow caught the attention of a homeless colony of Mexican free-tail bats... Every night at dusk, the families take to the skies in search of food. The spectacle of 1.5 million bats flitting forth at once looks a lot like a fast-moving, black, chittering river. It's become an Austin tradition to bring along a six-pack and cheer the bats as they head out to feast on an estimated 30,000 pounds of insects per night." —*www.lonelyplanet.com*

Beaumont

Largest Oil Strike—The Spindletop well, the largest oil strike in the United States, was drilled on January 10, 1901, four miles south of Beaumont. At the time, Russia was the world's largest oil producer, but the Spindletop output of 75,000 barrels equaled all the oil from eastern U.S. oilfields and half the U.S.'s oil consumption.

Dallas

"You want to know what Dallas is? Dallas is big hair, leased BMWs, and credit card millionaires." —Houston Texans fan Jeremy Radcliffe, in the August 19, 2002, *Sports Illustrated*

"Dallas is the most mythical city in Texas, with a past and present rich in all the stuff American legends are made of. Dallas is endlessly occupied with growth and status; it's a city known for its business acumen (especially in banking), its restaurants and its shopping. In the materially minded USA, Dallas stands tall as a paragon of conspicuous consumption." — *www.lonelyplanet.com*

"Stroll through Dallas' tree-lined streets, and you could easily be in Atlanta. The mood is Southern and very cosmopolitan. It's an image the city tries hard to cultivate. However, go next door to Fort Worth, and there's no denying you're in a former cowtown. Residents are proud of their wildcatting heritage and flaunt their cowboy style. Dallas-ites consider themselves way above that." —Geoffrey Precourt and Anne Faircloth in "Best Cities: Where the Living Is Easy," November 11, 1996, *Fortune*

El Paso

"Ice hockey, for El Paso, is just the tip of an iceberg. Thanks to all the Detroit, Saginaw, and Flint natives who have followed the auto industry south, this corner of the Southwest gets closer to Michigan every day. In fact, as America becomes more Latino, America's most Mexican city is becoming more like the Midwest." —*Wall Street Journal* reporter Joel Millman

"Juárez has grown much larger than El Paso—at night its lights stretch so far into Chihuahua that driving past it is like driving past L.A." —author Larry McMurtry, *Roads: Driving America's Great Highways*

Fort Worth
"Fort Worth is where the west begins, and Dallas is where the East peters out." —Fort Worth newspaper publisher Amon Carter

Houston
"Houston? All Houston's good for is traffic, humidity, and a ship channel that catches on fire." —Dallas Cowboys fan Chad Jones, in the August 19, 2002, *Sports Illustrated*

"It is not as beautiful as San Francisco; it does not carry itself with the stately being of Chicago; New Orleans is more picturesque, and New York is more visceral—but Houston is astir with the future." —Bill Moyers, *Listening to America,* 1971

"Despite its reputation as a gaudy boomtown that periodically goes bust, Houston seems ready to shrug off the troubles at three of its most visible corporate inhabitants—Enron, Compaq, and Continental—as though they were mere fender-benders on the way to church... Houston is beginning to mature, like a mining-camp madam who becomes a lady." —Brian O'Reilly, in the March 4, 2002, *Fortune*

"You can smell [the oil wells] from a distance. In the great desert of bare fields, this smell of factories and machines, this city smell, is the natural smell of the earth—the smell of the soil, of the sky, of the air. You can't even dream of being rid of it and recovering some lost purity: it's the fundamental truth. Infants in their cradles are already breathing it in those prefabricated houses lined up in rows on the stony ground, under the aegis of the tall iron towers. For many of the men who live here, life has had no other taste." —philosopher Simone de Beauvoir, March 27, 1947

"When oil reached $40 a barrel in 1981, Houston was awash in money as scores of happy Texans got rich quick; four years later, the price of oil plummeted to single digits and Houstonians got poor even faster. Glitzy but empty highrises stood next to giant construction holes that had to be filled back in when the financing ran out." —*www.lonelyplanet.com*

You've Gotta Have Heart—St. Luke's Episcopal Hospital in Houston was the site of the first artificial heart transplant on April 4, 1969, by Dr. Denton Cooley. The recipient died four days later.

Laredo

"Though the little border strip in Laredo is not radically different from what one would find in Del Rio, Juarez, Nogales, or Tijuana, here the palm trees give the scene a sort of dusty Middle Eastern tint. The street stops feeling like Texas and feels, for a moment, like Morocco." —author Larry McMurtry, *Roads: Driving America's Great Highways*

Mathis

"I had forgotten what summer is like in South Texas. It is so hot that the caliche streets turn into a fine white powder that swirls berserkly in the wake of the cars. The flat one-story buildings with their corrugated roofs collect dust and heat until they become chalky little ovens from which the Chicanos emerge in the evening to sit on the porch until dark." —from Bill Moyers' 1971 book, *Listening to America*

Texas City

Biggest Boom—One of the biggest explosions in the U.S. occurred in Texas City on April 19, 1947, when a fire aboard a French ship triggered an explosion, which in turn ignited a Monsanto chemical plant, which itself ignited an explosion at several oil refineries. The toll: 377 dead and 2,000 injured.

Utah

Quips & Quirks

When Brigham Young arrived in the Deseret Valley with the first Mormon settlers, he announced, "This is the place." At one point in the '90s, signs greeting those entering the state read, "Still the right place." On one sign, however, a graffiti artist commented on the state's conservatives' leanings by amending the sign to read, "Still the right-wing place."

"For a hundred miles west of Salt Lake City the country is common desert, dry, brown, full of sagebrush. Then gradually you come into the salt flats. You are taken by surprise. But little by little a feeling comes over you— a weird feeling of unworldliness. On either side, and ahead and behind, for miles and miles in every direction, the flat salt stretches to the very foot of the far-lying hills. The feeling is that of being in the center of a vast frozen lake. The salt resembles ice, and it's as level as a billiard table. Though the sun is shining, the sight makes you feel cold." —journalist Ernie Pyle, November 17, 1937

Bryce Canyon

"Just before cattleman [Ebenezer] Bryce died, he was approached to give a description of the canyon. They felt that his close association with it over so many years should bring forth a descriptive phrase that would live with the park for many years. They were right. Ebenezer thought a long time, and then he said: "Well, it's a hell of a place to lose a cow." —journalist Ernie Pyle, August 17, 1939

Salt Lake City

"I was in Salt Lake City once. It was closed." —Norman Fell in *Airport '75*, after hearing the pilot announce that the flight would be diverted due to a fog bank covering the entire west coast of the United States (a weather phenomenon that was a figment of the screenwriter's imagination).

"The puritanical, homogeneous white-bread community of Deseret—as Mormons used to designate their geographical base—is going multigrain, with people of different races, faiths and outlooks moving into the state." — Terry McCarthy, writing in the February 11, 2002, *Time*

"When followers of the Church of Jesus Christ of Latter-day Saints trekked westward in 1847 to escape persecution, their leader, Brigham

Young, put down his pack on the shores of the Great Salt Lake. Here, he believed, was a location so remote and unwanted that the members of his faith could finally live in peace." —*www.lonelyplanet.com*

"The city lies on the edge of a level plain as broad as the state of Connecticut, and crouches close down to the ground under a curving wall of mighty mountains whose heads are hidden in the clouds, and whose shoulders bear relics of the snows of winter all the summer long. Seen from one of these dizzy heights, twelve or fifteen miles off, Great Salt Lake City is toned down and diminished till it is suggestive of a child's toy-village reposing under the majestic protection of the Chinese wall... Salt Lake City was healthy—an extremely healthy city. They declared there was only one physician in the place and he was arrested every week regularly and held to answer under the vagrant act for having "no visible means of support." — Mark Twain in *Roughing It*

"The way in to the office of Gordon Hinckley, the president of the Mormon church, leads through long carpeted corridors with wood-paneled walls and security doors that swing open noiselessly with no visible movement from the guards. It is like walking into a David Lynch movie. In these hushed precincts, groups of gray-haired men in identical black suits pass by, beaming smiles like undertakers. Everyone is scrupulously polite, but as a visitor, one feels that one has been dropped into the middle of a plot, without knowing the beginning or the end." —Terry McCarthy, writing in the February 11, 2002, *Time*

Snowbird

"As storms drift across the dry Nevada desert, they are robbed of much of their water content. And when these same storms crash into the Wasatch Range, they are forced to pound Snowbird with the very lightest, and fluffiest powder in the Free World. Locals call it 'cold smoke.'" —*Skier's Journal*

Vermont

Quips & Quirks

"Vermont frightens me. The people who live there like it, and it is beautiful in a colossal sort of way. But in Vermont I can think only of the bitter winters, and the rocky hillsides, and the barrenness, and of people forever being beaten by nature, and of the ominous wind and hurrying snow clouds on a gray November afternoon, and of Calvin Coolidge, lying up there so alone amidst the bleak hills." —journalist Ernie Pyle, August 27, 1935

"No Vermonter would wish to deny that the state has, from the outset, carried particularism to the verge of intransigence; the motives only are in dispute. Vermont apologists have defended this attitude as the very essence of liberty. Outside observers have considered it as a consistent manifestation of unenlightened perversity." —*Vermont: A Guide to the Green Mountain State,* Federal Writers' Project, 1937

"Vermont is the only place in America where I ever hear *thrift* spoken of with respect." —a French friend of Vermont novelist Dorothy Canfield Fisher

"Vermont's twin cities [Barre and Montpelier] are natural and inevitable rivals, and offer a striking study of contrasts in appearance, character, and tone. Barre, forceful and arrogant, displays the haste and tension of a modern industrial community; Montpelier, serenely indifferent, is a true Vermont town, sleeping in the shadow of the hills. Barre may mock the Capital for being backward; Montpelier may scorn the Granite City as crude; but both are satisfied that in their very difference lies superiority." — *Vermont: A Guide to the Green Mountain State,* Federal Writers' Project, 1937

Burlington
"Sunset over the Bay of Naples is second only to a Champlain sunset seen from Burlington." —author William Dean Howells

Still Licking After All These Years—Though their factory is now in Waterbury (and open for tours), childhood friends Ben Cohen and Jerry Greenfield opened the first Ben & Jerry's ice cream stand in 1978 in a renovated gas station in Burlington; international food conglomerate Unilever bought the company in 2000.

Montpelier

"Its clean Doric simplicity emphasized in native stone, this Capitol has for Vermont something of the symbolic character which Edinburgh Castle holds for Scotland. From near-by hill roads in summer, the gold dome, gleaming through thick greenery, alone reveals the presence of a city." — *Vermont: A Guide to the Green Mountain State,* Federal Writers' Project, 1937

"There is an aloof, independent spirit about Montpelier and its people, a coldness bordering on indifference. While the town displays an interest in the cultural phases of life, it remains backward in several respects. Such an attitude, transcending normal Vermont conservatism, is perhaps traceable to the predominance of two bureaucracies [government and the insurance business], with the inertia and complacence inseparable from such a milieu." —*Vermont: A Guide to the Green Mountain State,* Federal Writers' Project, 1937

That's One Tough Town—Two heroes of the Spanish-American War were Admiral George Dewey and Captain Charles Clark, who defeated the Spanish fleet in the Philippines' Manila Bay and Cuba's Santiago Bay, respectively. Dewey was born in Montpelier and Clark lived there as an adult, leading humorists to refer to the war as "the conflict between the town of Montpelier and the kingdom of Spain."

Plymouth

"Those commentators who have expressed the belief that Calvin Coolidge's Yankee terseness, simple ways, and oft-repeated love of both the rigors and the beauties of his native State were a part of a sustained political pose are deluded by their own sophistication." —*Vermont: A Guide to the Green Mountain State,* Federal Writers' Project, 1937

Coolidge's First Oath of Office—In the early morning hours of August 3, 1923, during a visit to the house where he was born in Plymouth, vice-president Calvin Coolidge learned that President Harding had died in San Francisco the day before. Handily, Coolidge's father was a justice of the peace, and he administered the presidential oath of office to his son in the sitting room (Coolidge was again administered by oath several weeks later by a District of Columbia Supreme Court Justice).

St. Albans

"A place in the midst of greater variety of scenic beauty than any other I can remember in America." —minister and abolitionist Henry Ward Beecher

Woodstock

"Its instinctive reaction to change is negative: it has no factories and wants none; it saw its railroad discontinued without regret; it tenaciously cherishes its old covered bridge, picturesque but hazardous, at the west end of the village. If Woodstock sometimes places sentiment above progress, if it is—as its rustic neighbors say—too smug in its own well-being, it is perhaps by these very tokens a microcosm of the State to which, culturally, intellectually, and politically, it has contributed so much." —*Vermont: A Guide to the Green Mountain State,* Federal Writers' Project, 1937

Virginia

Quips & Quirks

The Most Unbalanced Ticket—Frequently presidential candidates will choose their vice-president to take into account geographical balance (hence the "Austin-Boston" tickets of Kennedy-Johnson and Dukakis-Bentsen), but the winners of the 1840 election—William Henry Harrison and John Tyler—were both born in Charles City County (though Harrison had served as governor of Indiana, he was actually nominated from Ohio).

Charlottesville

"I am as happy no where else and in no other society." —Thomas Jefferson, whose Monticello home is outside Charlottesville

Richmond

Presidential Endings—In Richmond's Hollywood Cemetery at 412 Cherry St., you'll find the gravesites of James Monroe, John Tyler, and Jefferson Davis.

Virginia Beach

"You probably think of Virginia Beach, Virginia, as a boardwalk town crammed with tasteless T-shirt shops and enough bars to keep the spring-break crowds happy. But don't be fooled: if you peel away the relatively tiny downtown strip, what's left is a thriving, family-friendly community that's diverse, welcoming and, in sports, take-your-breath-away gorgeous." —Sarah Mahoney in "Best Cities for Women," February 14, 2002, *Ladies Home Journal*

Warsaw

"You are now entering Warsaw—please set your watch back 150 years." —DJ Ray Arthur

Williamsburg

"Williamsburg is one of the sorriest shames to which I've ever fallen victim... Williamsburg couldn't help reeking of the fair and the movie studio, but after all, there is often poetry in fairs and movie studios. I don't know what cruel chance denied it any charm." —philosopher Simone de Beauvoir, April 6, 1947

Washington

Quips & Quirks

Presidential Seal—Washington is the only state named for a president, and it's the smallest state west of the Mississippi.

Seattle

"Let the word go forth at this time and place that Seattle is dark, ugly, rainy, unfriendly, and probably beyond saving." —columnist Emmett Watson, founder of the movement for Lesser Seattle, intended to thwart grand schemes of civic improvement

"Seattle is a mighty fine place. It remembers me a little of Duluth, Minn., built on the side of a mountain, with the bay below. The people out here are wonderful. Everywhere we have gone today, the people treated us very cordially and really seemed to take an interest. It is in marked contrast to the treatment one receives on the Eastern coast." —journalist Ernie Pyle, in a letter to his parents.

"It has its beautiful, soft downpour of steady rain, and its gray Saturday afternoons that are so comfortable. It has its ferryboats foghorning through the night, and its feeling of China and Alaska just out through the Sound, and it has Canada next door, and the mountains and skiing only forty miles away, and green thick forests and fish and bear and clear streams and industry and the Navy and the Japan Current and weather that never goes to zero." —journalist Ernie Pyle, February 10, 1937

"With the light falling across the buildings at certain times of the day, Seattle is as pretty as San Francisco, except that it does not have an old prison sitting in the bay." —from Bill Moyers' 1971 book, *Listening to America*

"People don't tan in Seattle, they rust." —bumpersticker, origin unknown

"Latte capital of the World,
Software Maker,
Unfurler of umbrellas,
Rider of bicycles and the Nation's Commercial Jet Builder;
Drizzly, hilly, self-aware,
City of the Big Shoreline:

"They tell me you love coffee and I believe them, for I have seen your sidewalk kiosks on every corner luring the passers-by.

"And they tell me you are fun to visit and my reply is: Yes, it is true all over town I have reasons to enjoy Seattle, then return to enjoy it again." — travel writer John Goepel

"Ever wondered whether caffeine is a viable substitute for sunshine? If so, Seattle is your kind of town. More than any other city in the region, Seattle epitomizes what people know of (and how they feel about) the Pacific Northwest. Never mind that its sunshiny days can be suicidally few, its residents (Chairman Bill [Gates], perhaps, excepted) are among the nation's most outgoing and outdoorsy. Sure, it had everybody wearing flannel shirts and whistling Nirvana for awhile, but consider also the good things it's given us: you can see the roots of America's microbrewing revolution in the bellies of many a Seattleite, and the city's chilly mornings had the espresso generation brewing long before Starbucks sold its first cup." — *www.lonelyplanet.com*

"Up to 1889—Seattle's first 20 years as an incorporated town—this burg was a pestilential hodgepodge, violence-ridden, rat-infested and poorly built upon low, tide-washed mudflats. The big blaze [of June 6, 1889, that destroyed most of downtown in 12 hours] gave civic boosters and planners a chance to completely reinvent Seattle, this time in fireproof brick, stone and iron." —travel writer J. Kingston Pierce in the July 1996 *Historic Traveler*

"Will the last person leaving Seattle please turn out the lights?" — billboard overlooking Interstate 5 south of the city erected in 1970 during the economic bust that followed Congress' scrapping the supersonic transport; ten years later, Bill Gates dropped out of Harvard, returned to his native Bellevue, and founded Microsoft

"Seattle may be the only place in America where athletic events are rarely called because of weather...after all, if games were canceled on account of wet weather, no one would ever play." —Geoffrey Precourt and Anne Faircloth in "Best Cities: Where the Living Is Easy," November 11, 1996, *Fortune*

"An incomparable natural setting, sheltered from harsh weather, peopled by friendly, intelligent folk with a proper respect for the landscape. It loves movies and you're seldom more than 100 yards from a good cup of coffee. So it rains some; big deal. That's why God made London Fog." —syndicated columnist Donald Kaul

Open for Business—Pike Place Market is the oldest continuously operated public market in the U.S., dating back to Saturday, August 17, 1907. Seattle city councilman Thomas P. Revelle suggested that space to set aside for farmers to set up wagons on Western Avenue above the waterfront in order to bypass wholesalers who paid a pittance for produce and then resold it at inflated prices.

Down And Out—Lumber used to be slid down the side of a hill above downtown Seattle to Elliott Bay, spawning the term "skid road." When the neighborhood went downhill, the term later was amended to "skid row" and eventually came to mean any hard-luck part of any city.

West Virginia

Quips & Quirks

Go West—West Virginia is the only state with west as a directional adjective and the only state with two panhandles.

The Broken State—During 1861, the first year of the Civil War, 25 counties voted to secede from Virginia, initially designating their new state Kanawha, after a local river.

World Travel Without Leaving—There are nineteen towns in West Virginia named after foreign cities: Athens, Berlin, Cairo, Calcutta, Geneva, Ghent, Glasgow, Killarney, Lima, London, Moscow, Odessa, Ottawa, Palermo, Rangoon, Santiago, Shanghai, Vienna, and Wellington.

More Than A Magazine—Union activist Mary Harris Jones began her career organizing miners in West Virginia in 1897; she was given her nickname "Mother" by the miners she was trying to protect (she also helped striking Pittsburgh railroad workers in 1877, Pennsylvania coal miners in 1899, and dressmakers in Chicago in 1924).

Natives—West Virginia natives include Tuskegee Institute president Booker T. Washington (Malden), Air Force General Chuck Yeager (Myra), gymnast Mary Lou Retton (Fairmont), and author Pearl Buck (Hillsboro).

Charleston

"Little houses in creamy colors—pink, red, white, bright yellow—look like the toys of wealthy children. They have tiny windows and doors, and the walls are as bright as cartoon drawings." —philosopher Simone de Beauvoir, April 4, 1947

"The most northern of the Southern cities and the most southern of the Northern cities." —Charleston Visitors Bureau (see also Baltimore, Md.)

Oak Hill

Enroute to a concert in Canton, Ohio, 29-year-old singer Hank Williams was found dead in the back seat of his Cadillac on New Year's Day, 1953, in Oak Hill.

Wisconsin

Quips & Quirks

"Why then was I unprepared for the beauty of this region, for its variety of field and hill, forest, lake? I think now I must have considered it one big level cow pasture because of the state's enormous yield of milk products. I never saw a country that changed so rapidly, and because I had not expected it everything I saw brought a delight." —John Steinbeck, *Travels with Charley*

Water, Water Everywhere—Door County has more miles of shoreline (250 mi.), more lighthouses (10), and more state parks (five) than any other county in the United States.

Green Bay

"On any given Sunday, the team and the town become one." — unknown ESPN sportscaster

Milwaukee

Beginnings—Actor Spencer Tracy was born in Milwaukee on April 5, 1900.

Wyoming

Quips & Quirks

"Many people in Wyoming refuse to boast about the grandeur of the state. They do not want to encourage a migration of newcomers. Privately they express the relief that the population in 1970 is smaller than it was [in 1960]. They want to keep the mountains and prairies and rivers as free as possible of the excrescence of urban progress. Tourists are welcome because they come and go, gracing the state with their money and their departure. I hardly blame the natives. I even hope they succeed." —from Bill Moyers' 1971 book, *Listening to America*

Afton

"Summer around here means two weeks of bad skiing." —Olympic wrestler and native Rulon Gardner

Casper

"Casper, the Friendly Host" —*the town's tourism slogan*

Oil Field Scandal—The great scandal of the Harding Administration revolved around members of the Cabinet leasing oil to private companies that was supposed to be kept in reserve for the military. The oil in question was stored at Teapot Dome, 38 miles northeast of Casper, and at Elk Hills near Bakersfield, California.

Yellowstone

"We enclose and celebrate the freaks of our nation and of our civilization. Yellowstone National Park is no more representative of America than is Disneyland." —John Steinbeck, *Travels with Charley*

Anywhere & Everywhere

"The Pacific Northwest remains determinedly downscale; people headed that way wear, almost always, a touch of gloom, but modest, civilized, Scandinavian-type gloom." —author Larry McMurtry, *Roads: Driving America's Great Highways*

"Settled as it was in large part from Massachusetts and Connecticut, New Hampshire shares with those parent States and with its side partners, Maine and Vermont, many basically Puritan characteristics—thrift, the will to work, individuality." —*New Hampshire: A Guide to the Granite State,* Federal Writers' Project, 1937

"The Mason-Dixon line is not just the boundary that settled an 18th century dispute between Maryland and Pennsylvania. It's a metaphor for a divided nation. In the 1820s, it began to be used in political speech for the North-South conflict. It was symbolically extended west along the southern boundaries of Ohio, Indiana, Illinois, then Missouri, and, as the nation's westering continued, on the straight line on the map now forming the northern boundaries of Oklahoma, New Mexico and Arizona, then projected on to include the population centers of southern Nevada and California. Since 1964, in 10 straight presidential elections no candidate from above the Mason-Dixon Line has won. In four of those elections both major party candidates were from the 20 states below the line. In the other six, candidates from below opposed candidates from above." —*Baltimore Sun* journalist Theo Lippmann Jr.

"There is one thing which America demonstrates invincibly, and of which I had been in doubt up till now: it is that the middle classes can govern a state. I do not know if they would come out with credit from thoroughly difficult political situations. But they are adequate for the ordinary run of society. In spite of their petty passions, their incomplete education and their vulgar manners, they clearly can provide practical intelligence, and that is found to be enough." —Alexis de Tocqueville, *Journey to America*

"Next to loneliness the national disease is homesickness. Just about everyone in America is from somewhere else, and many are from the farms and small towns which run through country music themes like aces in the hand of a Red River card shark. Charley Pride signs of a world 'full of country boys out on the street' who have come from 'the sticks of the country to the jungle of the city.' When he wonders 'could I live there any more,' he is speaking for half of the nation who left it and to the other half who would like to discover it. Country music has become the poetry of the search for an irrecoverable homeland." —from Bill Moyers' *Listening to America,* 1971

"Waiting for the bus to Oberlin in a large station posted with timetables, I'm fascinated by the list of names: Detroit, Pittsburgh, St. Louis... Hundreds of towns, hundreds of times the same town. You could travel day after day in the same bus, across the same plain, and you'd arrive each evening in the same town, which would have a different name every time." —philosopher Simone de Beauvoir, February 20, 1947

"In Italy, in Greece, in Spain, I've felt such regret that my condition as a traveler separated me from the inhabitants, who hardly travel at all. In contrast, the average American devotes a great part of his leisure time to driving along the highways. The gas stations, roads, hotels, and solitary inns exist only for the tourist and because of the tourist, and these things are profoundly part of America." —philosopher Simone de Beauvoir, March 11, 1947

"Hardly a day has passed that I haven't been dazzled by America; hardly a day that I haven't been disappointed. I don't know if I could be happy living here; I am sure I'll miss it passionately." —philosopher Simone de Beauvoir, May 19, 1947

"It's the emblematic American journey. In U.S. history there is always a tension between home and road. We talk a good talk about the joys of home, but the truth is we are obsessed with the road." —University of Tulsa professor of western American history James Ronda, speaking about the Lewis and Clark expedition in the July 8, 2002, issue of *Time*

"To me the summer wind in the Midwest is one of the most melancholy things in all life. It comes from so far, and it blows so gently and yet so relentlessly; it rustles the leaves and the branches of the maple trees in a sort of symphony of sadness, and it doesn't pass on and leave them still. It just keeps coming, like the infinite flow of Old Man River." —journalist Ernie Pyle, September 23, 1935

"Crossing state lines one is aware of this change of language. The New England states use a terse form of instruction, a tight-lipped, laconic style sheet, wasting no words and few letters. New York State shouts at you the whole time. Do this. Do that. Squeeze left. Squeeze right. Every few feet an imperious command. In Ohio the signs are more benign. The offer friendly advice, and are more like suggestions." —John Steinbeck, *Travels with Charley*

"In our Southern states there are a great many districts where white people cannot get acclimatized and where the blacks live and prosper. I imagine that in time the black population of the South, as it becomes free, will concentrate in that portion of the American territory, and the white population on the other hand will gradually move out. In that way a population will be formed entirely descended from the Africans, which will be able to have its own nationality and to enjoy its own laws. I can see no other solution to the great question of slavery. I do not think that the blacks will ever mingle sufficiently completely with the white to form a single people with them." —a Georgia planter named Clay, quoted in Alexis de Tocqueville's 1831 book *Journey to Americ*

"The Americans of the North are all full of intelligence and activity; the joys of the heart hardly play any part in their existence. They are cold, calculating, and reserved. The Americans of the South, on the other hand, are open and eager; habits of command give them a certain hauteur and an altogether aristocratic susceptibility to points of honour. They are much disposed to idleness and look on work as degrading." —a Louisiana planter named Brown, quoted in Alexis de Tocqueville's 1831 book *Journey to America*

"What distinguishes the north is the spirit of enterprise; what distinguishes the South is the spirit of chivalry. The manners of a Southerner are frank and open; he is excitable, even irritable, and very ticklish on a point of honour. The New Englander is cold, calculating, and patient. As long as you are staying with a Southerner, you are made welcome, and he shares all the pleasures of his house with you. The Northerner, when he has received you, begins to think whether he can do business with you." —a Baltimore lawyer named Latrobe, quoted in Alexis de Tocqueville's 1831 book *Journey to America*

"What I least understand in America is the nature and ways of activity of the political parties. In France, and elsewhere in Europe, society is divided by two or three important conceptions round which definite interests and emotions group themselves. In America I see nothing like that: one might say that there are nothing but coteries here and parties properly so called. Personalities are everything, and principles of little account." —Alexis de Tocqueville in his 1831 book *Journey to America*

Q: "How many [residents of the snobbish city of your choice] does it take to screw in a light bulb?" A: "None—the world revolves around them." (I originally heard this in reference to Palo Alto, the birthplace of Silicon Valley; I can poke fun at what's been called "Shallow Alto" because I grew up there..)

From the Internet: What Type of Person Reads What Newspaper...
- The *Wall Street Journal* is read by the people who run the country.
- The *New York Times* is read by people who think they run the country.
- The *Washington Post* is read by people who think they should run the country.
- *USA Today* is read by people who think they ought to run the country but don't really understand the *Washington Post;* they do, however, like their smog statistics shown in pie charts.
- The *Los Angeles Times* is read by people who wouldn't mind running the country, if they could spare the time, and if they didn't have to leave L.A. to do it.
- The *Boston Globe* is read by people whose parents used to run the country and they did a far superior job of it, thank you very much.
- The *New York Daily News* is read by people who aren't too sure who's running the country, and don't really care as long as they can get a seat on the train.
- The *New York Post* is read by people who don't care who's running the country either, as long as they do something really scandalous, preferably while intoxicated.
- The *San Francisco Chronicle* is read by people who aren't sure there is a country, or that anyone is running it; but whoever it is, they oppose all that they stand for. There are occasional exceptions if the leaders are handicapped minority feminist atheist dwarfs, who also happen to be illegal aliens from ANY country or galaxy and as long as they are Democrats.
- The *Miami Herald* is read by people who are running another country but need the baseball scores.

From The Internet: State Mottos...

Alabama: Hell Yes, We Have Electricity!

Alaska: 11,623 Eskimos Can't Be Wrong!

Arizona: But It's A DRY Heat

Arkansas: Literacy Ain't Everything

California: By 30, Our Women Have More Plastic Than Your Honda

Colorado: If You Don't Ski, Don't Bother

Connecticut: Like Massachusetts, Only The Kennedys Don't Own It—Yet

Delaware: We Really Do Like The Chemicals In Our Water

Florida: Ask Us About Our Grandkids

Georgia: We Put The "Fun" In Fundamentalist Extremism

Hawaii: Haka Tiki Mou Sha'ami Leeki Toru (Death To Mainland Scum, But Leave Your Money)

Idaho: More Than Just Potatoes...Well, Okay, We're Not, But The Potatoes Sure Are Real Good

Illinois: Please Don't Pronounce the "S"

Indiana: 2 Billion Years Tidal Wave Free

Iowa: We Do Amazing Things With Corn

Kansas: First Of The Rectangle States

Kentucky: Five Million People; Fifteen Last Names

Louisiana: We're Not ALL Drunk Cajun Wackos, But That's Our Tourism Campaign

Maine: We're Really Cold, But We Have Cheap Lobster

Maryland: If You Can Dream It, We Can Tax It

Massachusetts: Our Taxes Are Lower Than Sweden's (For Most Tax Brackets)

Michigan: First Line Of Defense From The Canadians

Minnesota: 10,000 Lakes...And 10,000,000,000,000 Mosquitoes

Mississippi: Come And Feel Better About Your Own State

Missouri: Your Federal Flood Relief Tax Dollars At Work

Montana: Land Of The Big Sky, The Unabomber, Right-wing Crazies, and Very Little Else

Nebraska: Ask About Our State Motto Contest

Nevada: Hookers and Poker!

New Hampshire: Go Away And Leave Us Alone

New Jersey: You Want A ##$%##! Motto? I Got Yer ##$%##! Motto Right Here!

New Mexico: Lizards Make Excellent Pets

New York: You Have the Right to Remain Silent, You Have The Right To An Attorney

North Carolina: Tobacco Is A Vegetable
North Dakota: We Really Are One Of The 50 States!
Ohio: At Least We're Not Michigan
Oklahoma: Like The Play, Only No Singing
Oregon: Spotted Owl...It's What's For Dinner
Pennsylvania: Cook With Coal
Rhode Island: We're Not REALLY An Island
South Carolina: Remember The Civil War? We Didn't Actually Surrender
South Dakota: Closer Than North Dakota
Tennessee: The Educashun State
Texas: Sí Hablo Ingles (Yes, I Speak English)
Utah: Our Jesus Is Better Than Your Jesus
Vermont: Yep
Virginia: Who Says Government Stiffs And Slackjaw Yokels Don't Mix?
Washington: Help! We're Overrun By Nerds And Slackers!
Washington, D.C.: Wanna Be Mayor?
West Virginia: One Big Happy Family...Really!
Wisconsin: Come Cut The Cheese
Wyoming: Where Men Are Men...and the sheep are scared!

From the Internet: You Live in the Deep South When...
You get a movie and bait in the same store.
"Ya'll" is singular and "all ya'll" is plural.
After five years you still hear, "You ain't from 'round here, are ya?"
"He needed killin'" is a valid defense.
Everyone has two first names: Billy Bob, Jimmy Bob, Mary Sue, Betty Jean, etc.

From the Internet: You Live in the Midwest When...
You've never met any celebrities, but the mayor knows your name.
Your idea of a traffic jam is ten cars waiting to pass a tractor.
You have had to switch from "heat" to "A/C" on the same day.
You end sentences with a preposition: "Where's my coat at?"
When asked how your trip was to any exotic place, you say, "It was different!"

Bibliography

Fiction

Barry, Dave, *Big Trouble*
McInerney, Jay, *Bright Lights, Big City*
Spencer, Scott, *Men in Black*
Wolfe, Tom, *A Man in Full*

Non-Fiction

De Beauvoir, Simone, *America: Day by Day* (Carol Cosman, trans.), University of California Press, 1999 (This is a translation from the original French of de Beauvoir's 1954 journal)

De Tocqueville, Alexis, *Journey to America,* J.P. Mayer, 1962 (This is a translation from the original French of de Tocqueville's journals of his 1831 trip to America; from these journals he wrote his seminal *Democracy in America)*

Dunlop, M.H., *Sixty Miles from Contentment: Traveling the Nineteenth-Century American Interior,* Basic Books, 1995

Elliott, Russell R., *History of Nevada,* University of Nebraska Press, 1973

Engel, Joel, *Rod Serling: The Dreams and Nightmares of Life in the Twilight Zone,* Contemporary Books, 1989

Gershkoff, Ira, and Trachtman, Richard, *Wild in the Streets: The Boston Driver's Handbook,* Addison-Wesley Publishing, 1982

Least Heat Moon, William, *Prairy Erth*

Lindberg, Richard C., *Quotable Chicago,* Wild Onion Books, 1996

McMurtry, Larry, *Roads: Driving America's Great Highways,* Simon & Schuster, 2000

Meyers, Jeffrey, *Scott Fitzgerald: A Biography,* HarperCollins, 1994

Moyers, Bill, *Listening to America,* Harper's Magazine Press, 1971

Pyle, Ernie (David Nichols, ed.), *Ernie's America: The Best of Ernie Pyle's 1930s Travel Dispatches,* Random House, 1989

Steinbeck, John, *Travels with Charley,* Viking Press, 1962

Trillin, Calvin, *U.S. Journal,* E.P. Dutton, 1971

World Wide Web

www.imdb.com The Internet Movie Database

www.lonelyplanet.com A Web site devoted to travel, run by the publisher of guidebooks for worldwide travel

Rinkworks.com/said/famous.shtml A Web site devoted to verbal flubs

With special thanks to my friends:

Selma Alabama	Helena Montana
Homer Alaska	Blair Nebraska
Gilbert Arizona	Henderson Nevada
Hope Arkansas	Meredith N. Hampshire
Tracy California	Elizabeth N. Jersey
Aurora Colorado	Anthony N. Mexico
Seymour Connecticut	Charlotte N. Carolina
Glen Burnie Delaware	Alexander N. Dakota
Orlando Florida	Delmar N. York
Perry Georgia	Willard Ohio
Pearl Hawaii	Ada Oklahoma
Jerome Idaho	Eugene Oregon
Niles Illinois	Chester Pennsylvania
Franklin Indiana	Warren R. Island
Harlan Iowa	Florence S. Carolina
Lawrence Kansas	Pierre S. Dakota
Murray Kentucky	Martin Tennessee
Eunice Louisiana	Austin Texas
Augusta Maine	Roy & Sandy Utah
Laurel Maryland	Milton Vermont
Beverly Massachusetts	Alexandria Virginia
Troy Michigan	Kent Washington
Albert Lea Minnesota	Ashley W. Virginia
Leland Mississippi	Kimberly Wisconsin
Hannibal Missouri	Cody Wyoming

If you'd like to contribute to the next edition of *Quip City*, send your quip, along with appropriate attribution (especially if it's not original) to howardbaldwin@pacbell.net.

Author's Biography

By age 16, author Howard Baldwin had visited 35 states (he still needs to hit Alaska, Minnesota, North Dakota, South Carolina, and West Virginia for a complete set). His first job out of college was at *Adventure Travel* magazine. Later he edited the *ASU Travel Guide,* a worldwide directory for airline employees. He's written travel articles for *Meetings 411, Newsday,* the Fort Worth *Star-Telegram, Pacific Travel News,* the inflight magazines of World Airways, Tower Air, and American Trans Air, and covered such wide-ranging destinations as New England, New Orleans, Las Vegas, Los Angeles, Hawaii, San Francisco, Morocco, the Philippines, and the Cayman Islands.